FRIGHTLOPEDIA

FRIGHT

AN ENCYCLOPEDIA OF

AND SPINE-CHILLING, FROM

WORKMAN PUBLISHING
NEW YORK

OPEDIA

VERYTHING Scary, Creepy,
ARACHNIDS TO ZOMBIES

by Julie Winterbottom

with contributions by Rachel Bozek

Illustrated by Stefano Tambellini

The authors and publisher disclaim responsibility for any adverse effects that result from using information in this book, including, but not limited to, being mistaken for a vampire, having spiders invade your toilet, and having nightmares about Mongolian death worms.

Copyright © 2016 by Julie Winterbottom

Illustrations © Workman Publishing Co., Inc.

Illustrations by Stefano Tambellini
Design by Becky Terhune and Jane Treuhaft
Editing by Justin Krasner
Production editing by Beth Levy

Library of Congress Cataloging-in-Publication Data is available.

ISBN 978-0-7611-8379-2

Workman books are available at special discounts when purchased in bulk for premiums and sales promotions as well as for fund-raising or educational use. Special editions or book excerpts can also be created to specification. For details, contact the Special Sales Director at the address below, or send an email to specialmarkets@workman.com.

Workman Publishing Co., Inc.
225 Varick Street
New York, NY 10014
workman.com

WORKMAN is a registered trademark of Workman Publishing Co., Inc.

Printed in the United States of America

First printing August 2016

10 9 8 7 6 5 4 3 2 1

ACKNOWLEDGMENTS

Writing a book can be scary—especially when it means having ghosts, zombies, and giant rats inhabit your mind for a whole year. Luckily, many people helped make the process of creating *Frightlopedia* less daunting.

Thanks to Stefano Tambellini for his wonderfully creepy illustrations; Jessica Facchini and Erin Petenko for their fastidious fact-checking; makeup artist Ramy for his ingenious instructions; and the fantastic team at Workman for their editorial and design wizardry: Justin Krasner, Becky Terhune, Jane Treuhaft, Beth Levy, Annie O'Donnell, and Bobby Walsh. Special thanks to Marilyn Recht for her eagle editorial eye.

Also, thanks to Brenda Bowen, David Rappaport, the staff at Steeplechase Coffee, and Stephen Wetta.—J. W.

And thanks to Ed, Mallory, Xander, the Bozek family, the Roswal family, Java Love, and the fine folks of PT. —R. B.

CONTENTS

INTRODUCTION

An 18-foot python just got loose from a pet store and is now slithering under the fence into your backyard.

In the middle of the night, as you're lying in bed, a strange, ghostly voice whispers your name again and again. And again.

A meteor just crashed into Earth and released a huge, pulsating blob of slime that is now consuming everything in its path.

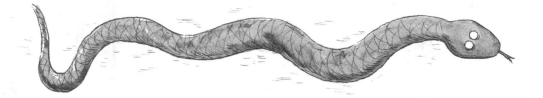

People have been scaring the pants—or loincloths and togas—off each other with stories like these for thousands of years. In fact, the ancient Romans told some of the first ghost stories, and they were a lot like the ones we tell today.

Being frightened, but knowing that you are not *truly* in danger, can feel deliciously good. It's what keeps thrill-seekers lining up for the amusement park ride that whips them around until they feel like a piece of wet spaghetti. It's what causes scary story lovers to ask to hear the same creepy legend again and again. It's what makes moviegoers rush to the theater to watch a film about a mutant monster brain that takes over the world. And chances are good that it's what brought *you* to this book.

You've come to the right place. In these pages, you will find stories about everything scary under the sun—and the full moon. You'll learn things you never knew about ghosts and mummies, aliens and werewolves. You'll encounter some real-life creepy creatures, petrifying plants, and ghastly places you never even imagined existed, like a wasp that turns prey into zombies, a plant that eats rodents, and an island that's overrun with thousands of snakes. You'll also learn how to make yourself—or your friends—look like a zombie, or better yet, a zombie that's been bitten by a vampire.

THREE THINGS TO KNOW ABOUT THIS BOOK

1. Everything is organized alphabetically. If a horde of zombies is at your front door right now and you need to know what to do *fast*, head straight to the *Z* section.

2. Being scared is fun, but being so scared you can't fall sleep at night is *not* fun. That's why every entry in this book has a score from 1 to 3 on the FRIGHT METER. This  will help you decide if something is the right amount of scary for you.

3. This book makes great scary reading, but it's not just for reading. There are lots of things to do and make, too. These are marked "Horrifying How-Tos." Some of these projects require help from an adult. They are labeled with the sign shown below. If possible, pick an adult who thinks it would be cool to see how you look with a fake vampire bite on your neck (and might even want one, too).

Ready to scare yourself and your friends silly? Turn the page,
IF YOU DARE . . .

AHH, ARACHNIDS!

SPIDERS

Maybe you're curled up reading a book. Maybe it's *this* book. Suddenly, out of the corner of your eye, you see something small and dark run across the page. It has lots of little legs. Hairy little legs. It moves so fast you're not sure you really saw it. You tell yourself it was just your imagination. But wait. There it is again! And now it's running up your arm. It's definitely a spider. And then it disappears again. Where did it go? Is it in your hair? Don't spiders love dark places like that? *AHHHHHHH!* You leap up screaming.

WHAT MAKES SPIDERS SO CREEPY?

They have eight angular legs that are often covered with hair. Most have eight eyes, which make them look like mini monsters close up—and make it easier for them to watch you. They hide in dark places, and when they come out, they dart around in unpredictable ways. They move fast, making it hard for people to keep track of them. (The giant house spider, one of the fastest in the world, can run almost two feet in one second!) Then there's the fact that spiders can walk on walls and ceilings, and they make sticky webs that cling to your skin—and let them dangle in front of you.

REASONS TO LOVE SPIDERS

The spiders on these pages are pretty scary, but that doesn't mean you should go around squashing every spider you see. Your chances of being hurt or killed by a spider bite are extremely small. In fact, most spiders are actually very helpful to people. They eat mosquitoes, and they help farmers control pests that damage crops. Some spider venom may even help treat cancer and other diseases.

On top of these facts, there are all the stories you hear about spiders. They like to bite people. And their bites can be deadly. At night, they crawl inside people's ears and lay their eggs. Even if these stories aren't actually true, if you're already afraid of spiders, it's easy to believe them.

SPIDERS THAT WILL MAKE YOU SCREAM

GOLIATH BIRDEATER TARANTULA

WHERE IT LIVES: South America

WHAT IT LOOKS LIKE: One of the biggest spiders in the world, this guy can grow to over 12 inches—big enough to span a dinner plate. Its body is covered in a thick layer of hairs, which makes it look extra creepy.

A Goliath birdeater tarantula devouring its unlucky prey.

THE SPIDER WEB THAT SWALLOWED A BUILDING

In 2009, workers at a wastewater treatment plant in Baltimore, Maryland, put out a call for "extreme spider help." Scientists who came to the rescue discovered that more than 107 million spiders had woven a four-acre web—that's the size of four soccer fields—inside the building. In some spots, more than 35,000 spiders were living in a space the size of a small desk. With water nearby, conditions were just right for the orb-weaving spiders to take up housekeeping together.

WHAT IT DOES: Although it's extremely rare, this spider has been known to catch (and eat) young birds—hence its name. More often, the hairy arachnid feeds on insects and the occasional rodent, lizard, or frog. It pounces on its prey, then sinks in its inch-long fangs and injects venom. This tarantula defends itself by flicking barbed hairs on its abdomen at intruders. The hairs irritate the victim's skin, nose, and eyes.

SCARIEST FEATURE: When threatened, the tarantula rears up on its hind legs and bares its fangs.

DANGER RATING: LOW
Although it looks terrifying, this spider is not dangerous to humans. Its bite feels no worse than a wasp sting, and its venom is harmless to people. Touching the tarantula's stomach hairs can temporarily irritate your eyes or cause a rash, though.

EXTRA CREEPY-CRAWLY FACT:
One of the largest Goliath birdeaters ever recorded was a

captive spider named Rosi that weighed over six pounds—comparable to a large Chihuahua.

BLACK WIDOW

WHERE IT LIVES: Throughout the world there are more than 30 species of black widow spider. In the United States, they are mostly found in Southern states.

WHAT IT LOOKS LIKE: The female of this shiny black spider breed has a red hourglass-shaped mark on her underside that warns victims "Time is running out." The males, which are relatively harmless, are smaller and lighter in color, and sometimes have red or brown spots or stripes on their backs.

WHAT IT DOES: A black widow snares insects in its web and injects them with venom that turns their insides into liquid, which the spider then slurps up.

SCARIEST FEATURE: A black widow's venom is believed to be 15 times more powerful than rattlesnake venom.

DANGER RATING: MEDIUM Black widows have powerful

SPIDER VS. BAT

In a contest between a spider and a bat, you would think the bat would win, but not if the spider is a certain large orb-weaver that lives in Costa Rica. These spiders weave gigantic webs that can measure five feet across. Occasionally the web snags a bat, and the spiders attack, kill, and devour the meaty meal.

venom, but they will bite only when disturbed (watch where you sit!), and only a large female can deliver enough venom to have any effect on a person. A bad bite produces severe pain, muscle cramps, nausea, and difficulty breathing.

EXTRA CREEPY-CRAWLY FACT:

Some female black widows devour the male spider after mating—which is where the name "black widow" comes from.

And when young spiderlings cannot find food, they sometimes eat their siblings.

SYDNEY FUNNEL WEB SPIDER

WHERE IT LIVES: Eastern Australia

WHAT IT LOOKS LIKE: Funnel web spiders have a hard, shiny shell on the front of their bodies with just a few hairs growing on it.

WHAT IT DOES: They build

funnel-shaped webs and hide in the narrow part until an unfortunate beetle or cockroach arrives at the web's wide inviting mouth. Then the spider rushes over and injects its victim with venom.

SCARIEST FEATURE: Considered one of the world's deadliest spiders, the male has venom that contains a chemical that acts on the nervous system and can kill a person in minutes.

DANGER RATING: HIGH
The Sydney funnel web spider can be very aggressive if threatened, and if you come near one your chances of being bitten are high. You can be treated with antivenom, but your best bet

AHHH! SCORPIONS!

Scorpions are arachnids, just like spiders, but when it comes to scariness, they're in a category all their own. They grab their prey—usually roaches and other insects—with nasty pincers and then use their mouths to inject digestive fluids that liquefy the victim's body for easy slurping. When threatened, scorpions will attack with the venom-filled stinger at the tip of their tail. A few dozen scorpions can deliver venom powerful enough to kill a person. Step carefully: These little creatures are found on  every continent except Antarctica! The most dangerous one of all is the Indian red scorpion, which resides in India and likes to live around people.

is to avoid getting too friendly with these spiders, especially the males, which are responsible for all known deadly bites.

EXTRA CREEPY-CRAWLY FACT:
Funnel web spiders make sudden lunges when they strike, and some people report that their fangs can penetrate soft shoes and fingernails.

OGRE-FACED SPIDER

WHERE IT LIVES: Africa

WHAT IT LOOKS LIKE: This sticklike spider has a face that is a perfect blend of cute and terrifying.

WHAT IT DOES: This spider doesn't wait for insects to come to it. It spins a web and holds it between its four front legs. Then, like an arachnid superhero, it stretches the web wide and hurls itself at its victim, covering the

Left: An ogre-faced spider, web held between its spindly legs, waiting to ensnare an unsuspecting victim.

Above: The spider's huge eyes make it look almost human.

insect with the sticky net before the unfortunate prey knows what hit it.

SCARIEST FEATURE: Its face. The ogre-faced spider's name says it all. Two of the spider's eight eyes are enormous and, combined with the massive fangs, make its face look oddly human yet absolutely macabre.

DANGER RATING: LOW
This spider is not very venomous. The main threat to people is that its face might give you nightmares for a few years.

EXTRA CREEPY-CRAWLY FACT:
It's hard to hide from this little ogre. Most spiders have very poor vision, but this one has military-grade optics and can see better than an owl at night.

AHH, ARACHNIDS!

FRIGHT METER

SPIDER IN THE TOILET

The unexpected sight of a spider in the toilet is enough to make most people scream—or at least decide that they can wait to use the bathroom. You can make your own fake spider and place it in the toilet bowl when you know your friend or sibling will be using the bathroom soon. Here's how.

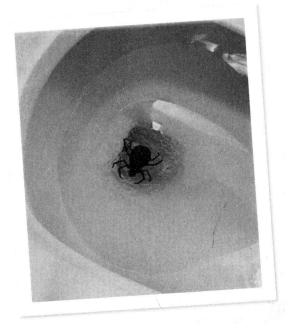

HORRIFYING HOW-TO

WHAT YOU NEED

- A piece of scrap paper
- Plastic wrap
- Scissors
- A black pen or marker or black fabric paint and a thin paintbrush

WHAT YOU DO

1. Place the paper on a table to protect it from the marker or paint. Cut out a small square of plastic wrap, about 2 inches wide, place it on the paper, and smooth it out so there are no wrinkles.

2. Use the black pen, marker, or a brush and fabric paint to paint a black spider on the plastic wrap. (You can also use the tip of the fabric paint bottle if it is pointed.) Use the drawing in the top right corner of this box as a model for your spider. If you use a pen to draw on the plastic, go over the drawing several times so it's dark black. You may want to practice drawing a spider on a piece of paper first to get the hang of it.

3. Let the spider dry completely. When it's absolutely dry, use the scissors to cut off the excess plastic wrap so you have a circle of plastic just big enough for the spider.

4. Carefully set the spider, paint/pen/marker side up, on the water in the toilet bowl. It should float.

5. Leave the bathroom and wait for your friend or sibling to go in. If all goes well, you should hear some screams.

BOO!

FRIGHT METER

People have been using the word *boo* or similar-sounding words, like *bo* and *boh,* to scare one another for more than 500 years. No one knows for sure, but the word *boo* may come from the old Scottish word *bu-man,* the name for an ancient devilish creature similar to a goblin.

In some countries, however, people use words that don't sound at all like *boo* to scare someone. This chart shows you how to say "boo" in 15 languages. Try some of these words on your friends to see which one gets the biggest jump.

LANGUAGE	PRONUNCIATION
English	Boo
Spanish	Boo or Ooh
French	Boo
Arabic	Boo
Bengali	Boo
Czech	Baf
Nepali	Boh
Japanese	Bah
Temne (spoken in Sierra Leone)	Boo-yah
Tibetan	Ah-BREE
Bulgarian	Ha
Swahili (spoken in Kenya)	O-ha
Hindi	Bhow
Portuguese	Bu
Chinese (Mandarin)	Hay

BURIED ALIVE

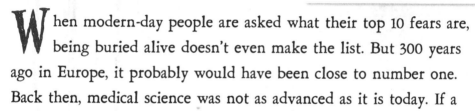

When modern-day people are asked what their top 10 fears are, being buried alive doesn't even make the list. But 300 years ago in Europe, it probably would have been close to number one. Back then, medical science was not as advanced as it is today. If a person appeared to stop breathing and had no noticeable heartbeat, he or she would be declared dead and quickly buried. Occasionally, a not-truly-dead person would end up being nailed into a coffin and placed six feet under.

In Scotland in the early 1600s, Marjorie Elphinstone was pronounced dead and promptly

The custom of holding a wake after someone dies comes from a tradition called "waking the dead." Someone would sit with the body from the time of death until the burial in case the person was unconscious, but not dead, and they happened to wake up.

buried. Grave robbers who dug up her coffin to steal her jewelry got the scare of their lives when they heard the "dead" woman groan! The robbers fled, while Marjorie dusted herself off and walked home.

In the 1800s, the fear of being buried alive became a near obsession for many people. To avoid that hideous end, some bought "security coffins" that allowed the "undead" to call for help by setting off firecrackers, sirens, and even rockets from inside. A doctor named Timothy Smith had a special tomb built for himself at a cemetery in Vermont with a window installed in the ground just above his head. People could peer in and check Smith's face to make sure he wasn't still breathing—or screaming.

Others arranged for their doctors to perform tests on their bodies right after they died to make sure there was no life left in them. The tests themselves were enough to scare someone to death: being stabbed with a red-hot iron or having boiling liquid poured on your skin. At least one person asked to be decapitated before burial—a surefire solution to the problem.

Today it's extremely rare for anyone to be buried alive. We have much better methods of determining whether or not someone is dead. But the fear of being buried alive—called taphophobia—hasn't died out completely. Not too long ago, in the 1990s, an Italian company offered a $5,000 casket with a two-way microphone/speaker and a survival kit that included an oxygen tank and a heartbeat detector, just in case . . .

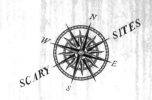
CAPUCHIN CATACOMBS

FRIGHT METER

It's considered rude to stare at strangers—if you are alive, that is. Dead people will stare at you shamelessly, through empty eye sockets, not caring if you stare back or turn away in horror. To experience one such staring contest firsthand, head for the Capuchin Monastery in Palermo, Italy. There you will find nearly 2,000 mummies patiently awaiting your gaze. They line the narrow stone halls, propped against the walls like people waiting (eternally) for a bus.

Many of the mummies still have their skin and hair, but it's their expressions that will really give you the creeps. Some have their jaws open as if in mid-scream; others display their rotted teeth in huge grins and appear to be clutching themselves in laughter. And then there are the outfits. These mummies are

dressed in their finest clothes—a bit tattered and stained, but what do you expect from people who haven't done laundry in about 200 years?

This huge gathering of eerily lifelike corpses is one of the scariest tourist attractions in the world. But scary is not what the monks who built the catacombs more than 400 years ago were going for.

The cemetery where they had been burying their dead had gotten full, so the monks dug a new crypt under their church. The cool, dry air in the crypt caused bodies to mummify naturally. The monks decided they liked the idea of preserving their brothers for eternity, and began draining and drying the corpses to preserve them better.

When the wealthy residents of Palermo heard about the

practice, they decided they, too, wanted to keep their lifelike appearance long after death. They considered it a status symbol, and they paid the monks to preserve their bodies and display them in the catacombs. On certain days, families would visit and hold the hands of their mummified relatives in prayer.

In 1881, the Italian government outlawed mummification at the monastery. These days the mummies provide a valuable record for historians about how people dressed and lived hundreds of years ago—they're sometimes called a "human library." But mostly they just stare...and stare.

CLAUSTROPHOBIA

FRIGHT METER

Y ou probably wouldn't want to spend more than a few minutes
in a packed elevator or have a closet door suddenly shut behind
you when you're
looking for a long-
lost sneaker way in
the back. You could
also probably find
better things to do
than get stuck in
traffic inside a tunnel.
It can be terrifying
to be trapped in a
small space—or any
space—with no way
out. You feel like you

have lost control because you cannot choose to leave. You may even start to wonder if you will be trapped forever or run out of air. People with claustrophobia—

While claustrophobia is the fear of enclosed spaces, the fear of being trapped is called cleithrophobia.

an intense fear of enclosed spaces—have an even harder time being stuck in small spaces. They may experience shortness of breath, feelings of extreme panic, and heart palpitations.

These real-life situations would give just about anyone a case of claustrophobia:

- In 1999, a man got stuck inside a New York City elevator for almost two full days with nothing to eat but Rolaids.

- In 2010, a woman in Paris, France, was trapped in her bathroom for 20 days when the door lock broke. She banged on the pipes to get the attention of neighbors in the apartment building, but they mistook the noise for home construction.

(The neighbors felt pretty bad when they realized their error!) The woman lived on nothing but water. Luckily, she did have a place to go to the bathroom.

- In 2014, a professional caver got trapped in Germany's deepest cave when he was injured by a falling rock. He had to wait 11 days for rescuers to get him out using about two miles of rope.

CLINKITY CLINK

FRIGHT METER

This ghost story is known as a "jump story." Read it a few times until you know it well. Then tell it to your friends in your most ghoulish voice. When you get to the end, jump at one of your listeners—who will then jump out of his or her skin! The story is adapted from an Uncle Remus story originally told by African Americans living in the southern United States in the 1800s. Have fun with the sound effects when you tell it.

An old lady who had lived by herself for as long as anyone could remember finally got sick one day and died. She had no family, so the neighbors had a coffin made for her. They placed it in the middle of her living room. Then they dressed her in her finest church dress and laid her in the box. There was one problem: She had died with her eyes open, and they were stuck that way—

looking everywhere but seeing nothing. One neighbor found two old silver dollars in the lady's house and placed them on her eyelids to keep them closed. That night, the neighbors sat up with her by candlelight so she wouldn't be alone.

The next day, the grave digger came to take her to the cemetery. As soon as he saw the shiny silver dollars on her eyes, he couldn't take his own eyes off them. He picked them up and felt how smooth and thick and heavy they were. "They're beautiful," he said to himself, "so beautiful."

Then he felt the dead woman staring at him. He knew she couldn't see, but with her eyes open the way they were, it felt like she was watching him hold the coins. He shut her eyes and put the coins back to keep them closed. But he couldn't resist. He grabbed the coins and stuck them in his pocket, then quickly hammered the lid shut on the coffin.

"Now you can't see a thing!" he said to her. He took her to the cemetery and dug her grave as fast as he could and buried her.

When he got home, he put the silver dollars in a tin box and shook it. They made a cheerful jangling sound, but the grave digger wasn't feeling cheerful. He couldn't stop thinking about those eyes staring at him.

When it got dark, a storm moved in. The wind started blowing. It whipped around the house, blowing in through the cracks and around the windows and down the chimney.

Buz-oooooo-o-o! it went. *Bizee, bizee, BUZ-OOOOOOOO-O-O!* The fire sputtered and flickered. The grave digger threw more wood on it, then got into bed and pulled the covers up to his chin.

The wind kept blowing and howling. *BUZ-OOOOOOOO-O-O! Bizee, bizee, BUZ-OOOOOOOO-O-O!* The fire flickered some more and threw evil-looking shadows on the walls. The grave digger watched them and pulled the covers tight around him. He lay there thinking about the dead woman's eyes staring at him. *BUZ-OOOOOOOO-O-O!* The wind got louder. The fire crackled and popped. The grave digger got more and more scared.

Then he heard another sound, a new sound. *Clinkity-clink, clinkity-clink.* It was the silver dollars jangling in the box.

"Stop!" yelled the grave digger. "Who is taking my money? Put it right back!"

But all he heard in response was the wind: *BUZ-OOOOOOOO-O-O!* and the firewood popping, and the coins going *clinkity-clink, clinkity-clink.*

Then he heard a voice way off in the distance. The voice cried, "Where is my money? Who's got my money? Whoooo? Whoooo?"

Now the grave digger was really scared. He got up and piled all the furniture against the door. He put a heavy iron frying pan over the tin box. Then he got back in bed and covered his head with the blankets.

But the coins jangled louder than ever: *Clinkity-clink, clinkity-clink.* And the voice screamed, "Give me my money! Who's got my money? Whoooo? Whoooo?"

The grave digger pulled the covers even tighter, but it didn't help. He trembled and shook and cried out, "Oh, Lordy, Lordy!"

Suddenly the front door flew open. The grave digger almost had a heart attack. In walked the ghost of the dead woman. Her eyes were wide open, looking everywhere and seeing nothing. The wind howled. *BUZ-OOOOOOOO-O-O!* The money went *clinkity-clink, clinkity-clink.* The fire snapped and popped, and the ghost

of the dead woman shrieked, "Where is my money? Who has my money? Whoooo? Whoooo?" And the grave digger could do nothing but moan, "Oh, Lordy, Lordy!"

The ghost could hear the sound of her coins going *clinkity-clink, clinkity-clink* in the tin box, but her dead eyes couldn't see where the box was. She reached out her arms and tried to find it.

[Note: At this point in the story, stand up with your arms out in front of you and start moving them around.]

The wind was still howling. *Bizee, bizee, BUZ-OOOOOOOO-O-O!* And the money jangled, *clinkity-clink, clinkity-clink!* And the fire snapped and popped. And the grave digger moaned, "Oh, Lordy, Lordy!" And the ghost cried, "Give me my money! Who's got my money? Whoooo? Whoooo?"

[Note: Now jump at one of your listeners and scream:]
YOU'VE GOT IT!

CREEPY CREATURES

CROCODILES

FRIGHT METER

There are 13 species of crocodile in the world, and most of them are sweetie pies compared to the saltwater croc. This enormous meat-eating reptile has the strongest bite of any animal in the world. When it clamps down on its prey with its 70 long, extremely sharp teeth, there is no escaping. As one biologist put it, "It is a one-way street between the teeth and stomach."

The saltwater croc is the biggest, most aggressive crocodile, and some say it's the animal most likely to eat a human. Commonly found in Australia and islands in the Pacific

Ocean, saltwater crocs are monstrously huge. They average 17 feet long (about the length of a minivan), but some grow to be 23 feet

long and can weigh more than a ton.

Saltwater crocodiles are extremely patient and effective killers, and will attack anything from a huge water buffalo to a shark. Their method is sneaky: They hide under the surface of the water with only their eyes and nostrils poking out. And wait. And wait. When the prey comes near, the crocodile explodes out of the water, grabs the victim in its powerful jaws, drags it underwater, and holds it there until it drowns. If necessary, the saltwater crocodile can hold its breath for an hour.

A victim's chances of wriggling free are close to zero thanks to the croc's powerful jaws, which exert a record-breaking 3,700 pounds of pressure on the victim's flesh. By comparison, the average pressure of a human bite is a wimpy 100 to 150 pounds.

A crocodile's hearing is so good that she can listen to her babies calling from inside her eggs.

I CAN'T GET TO THE PHONE RIGHT NOW

Crocodiles don't chew their food; they swallow it whole or in large chunks. At a wildlife park in Ukraine, a croc accidentally swallowed a phone dropped by a visitor. It could be heard ringing inside the animal's stomach.

SCARED TO. . .
DEATH!

FRIGHT METER

You're concentrating very hard on your homework—or a video game—and someone comes up behind you and taps you on the shoulder. You leap four feet in the air and yell, "You scared me to death!" It's a common expression. But is there any truth to it? Can a person actually die of fright?

The short answer is, yes. But don't let that scare you to death. It's very rare, but it is possible for strong emotions like fear to trigger a heart attack. When you get extremely scared, your body produces a chemical called adrenaline that makes your heart beat faster so it can pump more blood and help you run away from danger faster if you need to. But lots of adrenaline can be toxic to the heart and, in rare cases, cause death. That's what police said happened to a 79-year-old woman in Charlotte, North Carolina, after a bank robber broke into her home and tried to hide there. He never touched the woman, but she apparently died of a heart attack triggered by fear.

Other powerful emotions—including extreme happiness—can have the same effect. A man who played golf his whole life was in the middle of a game when he hit a ball over a slight hill. He couldn't see where it went. When he and his partner walked over to look, they saw that it was in the hole. The golfer was ecstatic. He turned to his partner and said, "Wow, I hit a hole in one. I can die now." And he did.

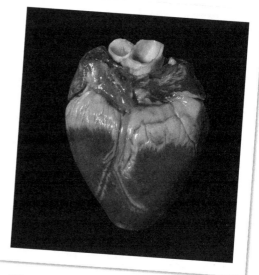

Although the heart is one of the hardest-working organs in the human body, sometimes it's no match against fright.

EVIL SCIENTIST

FRIGHT METER

There is a long tradition of fictional evil scientists doing experiments that unleash scary new life-forms into the world. You can keep the tradition going—and scare your friends—by filling jars with creepy "specimens" and telling visitors that they were left in your house years ago by the descendants of Dr. Frankenstein.

HORRIFYING HOW-TO

ADULT
HELP

WHAT YOU NEED

- Glass jars of various sizes, ideally with wide mouths and smooth sides
- Weak iced tea or lemonade (or other light brown or yellowish liquid)
- Paper, tape, scissors, and pen
- Kitchen knife
- Any of the following food items, depending on how many specimen jars you want to make:
  > Cauliflower (cooked is best)
  > Mozzarella cheese (the whole cheese, unsliced)
  > String cheese (white)
  > Canned mushrooms (look for them in the canned vegetables aisle at the supermarket)
- Flashlight
- An adult to help

WHAT YOU DO

1. Prepare the jars

   Remove any labels from the jars by soaking them for 5 to 10 minutes in hot (not boiling) tap water and then sliding off the labels.

2. Prepare the ingredients for each jar

   - To create cauliflower "brains": Break off a few large pieces of cauliflower—about the size of your fist is ideal, but they should be small enough to fit in the jar you are using. Ask an adult to help you boil, steam, or microwave the cauliflower until it is tender but not mushy—about 4 to 5 minutes. When it's done, drain off the hot water and cover the cauliflower with cold water. Then place one or more pieces in a jar and fill it

-CONTINUED-

with the light brown or yellow liquid (iced tea works well). Add water to lighten the color if necessary.

- **To create "stomach" or "spleen" (or other organs):** Ask an adult to help you cut several ½-inch-thick slices of mozzarella cheese across the widest part of the cheese. Use your finger to stretch each slice a little to create slight holes and texture. Place the slices in a jar and fill with brown or yellowish liquid.

- **To create "intestines":** Use your fingernail to scoop out the ends of three or four string-cheese sticks so they aren't completely square and look like they could be hollow inside. Then curve each one and place it at the bottom of the jar, one on top of the other, so they look like coiled intestines. Add liquid.

- **To create "monkey hearts":** With an adult's help, cut the stems off 5 or 6 mushrooms so you just have the tops left. Place the tops in a jar and add liquid.

3. Experiment!

You can come up with your own ideas for things that will look like specimens when you put them in pale-colored "preservative" liquid. Here are some suggestions to get you thinking:

- Chicken livers or other leftover parts from a whole chicken.

- Hard-boiled egg. Remove the yolk and slice the white part in half. You can combine this "organ" with the string-cheese intestines.

- Cooked sausage. Bend the sausages so they look like fingers or intestines.

4. Make labels for the jars

For each specimen, make up your own creepy name or choose from the list on the right. Write or print the names on white paper, cut them out, and tape the labels on the front of the jars. You can even dab a little iced tea on each label to make it look old.

5. Hide the jars

Place the jars in a row on a dark shelf in the basement, attic, or a closet. Choose a place where they might have gone unnoticed for many years.

6. Invite your friends over

When your friends are at your house, tell them a story about scientists who used to live in your house and got thrown in jail for trying to create new life-forms. Explain that you found some of the creepy experiments in the basement (or attic/

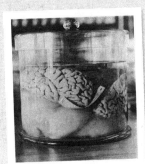

SPECIMEN NAMES

Goat Brain, 1980

Stomach #4

Intestine

Found in Sheep's Kidney

Gift of Dr. V. Hackenberg

Revivified Stomach

Removed from Human Brain, 1984

Feline Intestines #13

Black Widow Spider Eggs

Partial Fingers

Unknown Parasite #5

Monkey Hearts

Mutated via Radiation

closet), and offer to show them to your friends. Bring a flashlight and don't turn on any other lights. Spend a little time "searching around" for the jars. When you find them, shine the flashlight slowly from one to the next.

Here's an example of the kind of story you might tell:

"*In the 1980s, a husband and wife who were scientists lived in this house. At night, they performed secret experiments to try to create new creatures and bring the dead back to life. One day a neighbor was putting out her garbage when she noticed something that looked like a brain squirming around in the scientists' garbage can. She called the police, and they came, searched the house, and arrested the couple.*

About a year ago, I was playing in the basement [or attic or closet] and I found these old specimen jars that still have their experiments inside. They have been soaking in preservative stuff for years. I don't even have the nerve to touch them. But sometimes I dare myself to go look at them. Want to see them? I think some of them are not completely dead. . . ."

FAKE BLOOD
AND FAKE WOUND

FRIGHT METER

Fake blood and a fake wound make any Halloween costume look
a lot scarier, and are also perfect for freaking out your friends
at any time of year.
Here's how to
make both.

HORRIFYING HOW-TO
fake blood

WHAT YOU NEED

- Small mixing bowl
- Measuring spoons
- Fork or whisk
- Water
- Corn syrup
- Red food coloring
- Blue or green food coloring
- Cornstarch
- An adult to help

WHAT YOU DO

1. In the mixing bowl, combine 1 tablespoon of water with 3 tablespoons of corn syrup. Mix well with fork or whisk.

2. Add red food coloring one drop at a time until the liquid is very red.

3. Add blue or green food coloring one drop at a time to darken the red so it's the color of blood. You may need only one drop.

4. Add ½ teaspoon of cornstarch and use the fork or whisk to mix it in. If the blood is too thin, keep adding cornstarch until it's the right thickness. (If you accidentally make it too thick, just add drops of water and mix until it's right.)

5. Use your fake blood to make your Halloween costume more gory, or use it for other scary projects. Just make sure you don't get it on anything important, like the rug or the dog.

If you need more fake blood, double or even triple the amounts suggested throughout the recipe.

HORRIFYING HOW-TO

fake wound

Sometimes putting a fake gash on your forehead with no other costume is the scariest thing you can wear on Halloween—at least according to makeup artist Ramy, who gave us these tips for making a killer fake wound.

WHAT YOU NEED

- Theatrical wax (Buy this at a local party supply store or order it online with the help of an adult.)
- Moisturizer or lotion
- A small spatula
- Fake blood (see recipe on facing page)
- An adult to help

WHAT YOU DO

1. Take a little piece of theatrical wax (about the size of a small marble) and roll it between your hands until it's the shape and length of a small worm.

2. Press the theatrical wax onto your hand, forehead, or wherever you want the wound to be. Flatten the wax.

3. Apply moisturizer or lotion to the wax and blend it in.

4. Take the small spatula and "cut" a line down the center of the wax in a straight line. This cut is the wound.

5. Apply fake blood to the cut. You can make the fake blood look like it's dripping out of the wound by drawing squiggly lines from the cut to the surrounding skin.

GHOSTS

FRIGHT METER

Have you ever seen, or felt, or smelled, a ghost? Do you know people who say they have? Reports of ghosts have been around for almost as long as humans.

Ghosts are thought to be the spirits of dead people who have returned to earth (or refused to leave in the first place), usually because they are angry or sad about something that happened to them when they were alive or because they want to help loved ones they have left behind.

People who say they have seen ghosts often describe them as a glimmer of light or a nearly transparent blur. Sometimes they are invisible and reveal themselves through strange sounds, a draft of cool air, or a mysterious smell.

In the Middle Ages, French alchemists thought they could create ghosts out of human blood. They claimed that when they heated blood samples in charcoal burners, ghostly shapes appeared in the steam.

GHOST LIGHTS

Ghost lights are mysterious orbs of light that appear over bogs and marshes. Also known as will-o'-the-wisps, they are thought to be mischievous spirits of the dead that try to lead travelers into dangerous areas. Some scientists have another explanation: They say the flickering lights could be swamp gases catching fire or the effects of creatures like fireflies that glow in the dark. Long ago, similar lights were sometimes reported in cemeteries. Known as "corpse lights," they may have been caused by gases that seeped out of bodies buried in shallow graves. Eek!

ARE GHOSTS REAL?

As many as two out of five Americans say that they believe in ghosts. One in five say they have encountered one. In Asia, the belief in ghosts is thought to be even more widespread. But some people, known as skeptics, would say that while people may *think* they have seen (or felt or heard) a ghost, there is almost always a real-world explanation for what happened. (See "If It's Not a Ghost, What Is It?" on page 52.)

What do you think? Do you believe in ghosts? Or are you like the French noblewoman who once declared, "Do I believe in ghosts? No, but I *am* afraid of them."

A GUIDE TO GHOSTS

Ghosts come in many varieties and have different purposes. Here is a quick guide to common spirits:

HAUNTING GHOSTS

These spirits are said to return to the same place again and again and are usually seen there by different people. Haunting ghosts may return because of a wrongful death or unfinished business.

A small village in India holds a monthlong Ghost Fair every year. Thousands of people come to get rid of evil ghosts that they claim have possessed them.

GHOSTS OF THE LIVING

These ghosts look like someone who is still alive. Some people think they appear as a warning that the living person is in trouble or near death.

MESSENGER GHOSTS

These ghosts have a mission. They come to deliver a message or warning from someone who is dead. They rarely speak, but instead make gestures or signs.

POLTERGEISTS

German for "noisy spirits," these invisible phantoms are known for knocking on walls and making

objects fly through the air and break. Poltergeist activity often takes place when teenagers are present. Whether that's because they attract these spirits or are just good at pranks, no one knows for sure.

COLD-SPOT GHOSTS

These unseen ghosts may appear as columns of cold air that people feel as they walk through certain haunted buildings.

SPIRIT VOICES

These are mysterious voices said to appear without explanation on voice messages, the radio, or digital recordings made in haunted places.

FAMOUS GHOSTS

Like people, some ghosts become famous. These four ghosts may or may not be real, but they certainly are well-known.

ANNE BOLEYN: *BEHEAD* OF HER TIME

The Tower of London in England is famous for its many ghosts. For hundreds of years, people accused of crimes were executed there. One of the most famous victims was Anne Boleyn, who was falsely accused of betraying her husband, King Henry VIII,

and beheaded at the Tower in 1536. Ever since, her ghost has been reported walking through the area, sometimes carrying her head in her arm. If you believe in ghosts, it's a perfect case of a spirit that can't find peace because of a wrongful death.

THE PHANTOM FOWL

Not all ghosts are the spirits of people. The phantom of a frozen chicken is said to haunt a park in London, England. The story goes that on a bitterly cold day in April 1626, the scientist Sir Francis Bacon was taking a carriage ride through Pond Square with his friend Dr. Witherbone. The two were discussing ways to preserve food. Bacon suggested using snow as a type of refrigeration (refrigerators had not yet been

invented). His friend laughed at the idea, but Bacon insisted on conducting an experiment then and there. He stopped the carriage and ran to a house, where he bought a hen. He had it prepared at a nearby butcher store, then packed it in snow and placed it in a bag, creating the world's first intentionally frozen chicken.

Bacon never got to report on his experiment. He came down with pneumonia and died a few days later. The chicken, however, was not ready to move on.

Soon people reported hearing the eerie sound of a chicken screeching near Pond Square. Others said they saw a half-plucked chicken running around the park. The sightings continued for years, but whenever someone tried to get near the bird, it would vanish.

The most recent reported sighting was in 1970, when a couple kissing in a doorway was interrupted by the ghostly sound of a squawking fowl. It gave them goose bumps . . . or more accurately, chicken bumps.

GETTYSBURG GHOSTS

People seeking out spirits often visit battlefields because ghosts are believed to haunt scenes of death. One of the most fertile grounds for ghost sightings—or for people's imaginations—is Gettysburg, Pennsylvania, where one of the bloodiest battles in the American Civil War took place.

Some Gettysburg visitors claim to have seen and even spoken to phantom soldiers who roam the battlefield. Others report hearing the sounds of cannon fire and the screams of injured fighters. People also say they have seen lights flashing in the mist along the path Confederate soldiers took to a hilltop battle.

While some insist these hauntings are all real, others say the mist and fog that often shroud the Pennsylvania battlefield make it easy for people's eyes to play tricks on them.

THE VANISHING HITCHHIKER

It's generally not a good idea to pick up hitchhikers—especially if the hitchhiker is a phantom.

Stories of a hitchhiker who gets into a car (or in earlier times, a horse-drawn wagon) and then disappears into thin air have been told around the world for centuries. In modern American versions, a driver gives a lone hitchhiker a ride at night. After traveling a few miles, the driver turns around to ask the passenger a question, only to find that the person has vanished. The driver continues on to the house where the hitchhiker asked to be dropped off, and is told that the person died many years ago in a car accident. Or, the driver stops at the cemetery the passenger wanted to visit and finds a piece of her clothing draped over a tombstone with her name on it.

Most people consider this well-traveled tale an urban legend. Whether or not it's true, it certainly has gotten a lot of mileage.

GHOST HUNTERS

Ghost hunting is a popular hobby, and thousands of people all around the world belong to ghost-hunting societies. They visit supposedly haunted buildings hoping to spot a ghost or, better yet, photograph one with an infrared camera.

Ghost hunters are hardly new, though. One of the first, Joseph Glanvill, investigated a poltergeist for the King of England in the late 1600s. A few centuries later, when interest in ghosts soared, ghost hunters used nothing fancier than their eyes, ears, a notebook, pen, camera, compass, and string or wire to try to determine if a building or location was haunted.

These days, some ghost investigators use expensive high-tech equipment, from laser thermometers to electromagnetic-field meters to electronic security systems. Most of these ghost hunters call themselves "paranormal investigators." They usually start with a belief in ghosts, and sometimes use nonscientific aids, conducting séances or contacting psychics who say they can summon ghosts.

A few ghost investigators take a more scientific approach, though. They start by looking for all the possible natural explanations for a haunting. They study maps to locate underground streams, tunnels, mines, and other features that might affect a building. They spend many nights and days in a building, making lots of recordings and observations and tracking the source of every sound or movement they detect. This type of ghost hunting can be disappointing if you are hoping to find a ghost. So far it has not produced any evidence of a real haunting.

IF IT'S NOT A GHOST, WHAT IS IT?

Ghost hunters and others who use scientific methods to investigate reportedly haunted locations often discover that the "ghost" can be explained by common household noises or other natural events.

BAD VIBRATIONS

Strong vibrations produced by thunder, traffic, or certain appliances can affect people's vision and make them see things that aren't really there—things that seem like ghosts.

That's what happened to a scientist named Vic Tandy. He was working in his lab one day when he saw a mysterious gray shape sit down next to his desk and then disappear. Tandy recalled other workers saying they had seen dark figures in the same area. They also complained of feelings of dread and the sensation of being watched. Being a scientist, Tandy decided to investigate. He discovered that an exhaust fan was sending out powerful vibrations in that part of the building—strong enough to make people's eyeballs vibrate and cause them to see things that weren't there. Vibrations can also affect people's stomachs, causing feelings of fear and anxiety. Tandy turned off the fan and, sure enough, the "ghosts" disappeared.

STRANGE ENERGY

Electromagnetic waves are another kind of energy that may make places seem haunted. These waves can come from natural sources, like the Earth's magnetic field or the buildup of electricity during a thunderstorm, or they can come from microwave ovens, TVs, and many other appliances. Some scientists

Household Happenings

The sound of ghostly footsteps in the middle of the night . . .	COULD BE	. . . the house settling into its foundation.
The mysterious knocking on a wall . . .	COULD BE	. . . old plumbing pipes banging.
The shriek and moans coming from the attic . . .	COULD BE	. . . the wind blowing around the corner of a building.
The door that opens on its own . . .	COULD BE	. . . the movement of water underground that shakes the house.
The cold spot in a room . . .	COULD BE	. . . dry air entering a humid room, which feels cool against your skin.
The lights going on and off by themselves . . .	COULD BE	. . . glitches in the electrical wiring.
The sound of someone running through the house . . .	COULD BE	. . . rats (which, come to think of it, might be scarier than ghosts).

think these energy waves can stimulate people's brains so they sense a ghostly presence and feel frightened or anxious. When scientists measured the electromagnetic waves in the famously haunted Hampton Court Palace in England, they found the highest levels in the spots with the most ghost

Electromagnetic waves are off the charts at the haunted Hampton Court Palace, the alleged home of various restless spirits.

sightings. Of course, those who believe in hauntings say that ghosts are responsible for the change in energy levels.

IT'S A GAS!

A more dangerous explanation for ghost sightings is the poisonous gas carbon monoxide. Some household furnaces produce small amounts of this deadly gas. Normally the gas exits the house through vents. But if the gas accumulates inside a house, it can cause headaches, dizziness, nausea, and (this is where ghosts come in) feelings of dread and hallucinations.

TRICKS OF THE MIND

Maybe it's Halloween night, and you look up at a tree and think you see a gruesome face peering out of the trunk. It turns out just to be shadows on the bark. Some skeptics think that this is what happens when people see ghosts—especially if they are in a place they have been told is haunted. You see a shadow or a reflection of light or an insect flying by and your mind interprets it as a ghost.

WAKING DREAMS

These happen when a person wakes up suddenly. For a few seconds, their brain is still in a dreaming state but their body is awake. It's hard to tell the difference between a dream and reality during this brief time, and if you are dreaming about a person, it may suddenly seem as if he or she is in the room with you—like a ghost.

GHOSTS AROUND THE WORLD

FRIGHT METER

Ghosts get around. Just about every place in the world has its own version of spirits returned from the dead. Some are scary, but others are playful and even helpful.

Here are just a few of the ghosts that haunt people across the globe.

THE BLUE-HAIRED GHOST

In the town of Rimini on the coast of Italy, a castle is said to be haunted by the ghost of a girl who cries "Mama!" on June 21 of every fifth year. The story goes that hundreds of years ago the

girl's mother tried to darken her daughter's snow-white hair, which people believed was a sign she was a demon. The girl's hair ended up looking blue, so she was nicknamed Azzurrina, meaning "Blue-Haired Girl." On the 21st of June, Azzurrina disappeared while playing in the castle basement. Her body was never found, but centuries later, her ghost still haunts the castle.

THE GHOST WITH HALF A BODY

In Tanzania, people once believed in a ghost called a *kinyamkela*. It lived in the hollow of a tree and was invisible most of the time. When it did appear, it looked like half of a human body, with one leg, one hand, one eye, and one ear. The *kinyamkela* had a temper.

If you took bananas from its tree, for instance, it would shower you with stones and human bones and threaten to kill you. But if you brought it some replacement food, it was willing to forgive.

THE FISH-LOVING GHOST

In parts of India and Bangladesh, a *mechho bhoot* is a brawny male ghost that adores fish and often steals them from fishermen. The greedy ghost is also known to enter people's homes and run off with freshly prepared meals. If you refuse to give this ghost food, it will enter your body and make you vomit. Maybe handing over the fish is a good idea.

THE HAIRY, HELPFUL GHOST

A *domovoi* is a friendly ghost with a long beard that lives in Russian homes. *Domovois* help with chores and protect families from evil spirits. But sometimes they get angry—especially if they witness sloppy housekeeping or bad language. Then they behave like poltergeists, knocking on walls, making objects rattle, and leaving muddy footprints all over the house.

THE ANGRY GHOST

In Japan, *onryō* are angry ghosts who seek vengeance on those who wronged them. Sometimes they kill their enemies and remove their spirits; other times they get revenge by causing earthquakes and other natural disasters. One of the most famous *onryō* is Oiwa, the ghost of a woman whose husband betrayed her and then tried to poison her. Oiwa wears a white dress and has long ragged hair. Her left eye droops down her face, and she is partly bald (damage caused by the poison). Rather than kill her husband, she torments him by following him everywhere.

THE HUNGRY GHOST

In some Chinese religions, people who behave badly when they are alive are believed to return to Earth as *egui* or "hungry ghosts" after death. These ghosts are in a terrible bind: They crave food, but they cannot eat. Some have flaming mouths that set food and drink on fire. Others have mouths the size of a pinhole and pencil-thin throats that prevent them from being able to swallow.

THE WEEPING GHOST

In Mexico, a ghost known as La Llorona (the Weeping Woman) is said to roam the countryside, crying desperately as she searches in vain for her children. There are many versions of the legend. Some say that La Llorona was once a beautiful woman who went mad when her husband rejected her. She drowned her children in revenge. Horrified by what she'd done, she proceeded to drown herself, too. Her ghost wanders eternally, weeping. Men who follow her end up disappearing forever—it's La Llorona's revenge against her husband.

THE SCREAMING GHOST

Legend has it that in the 1860s, the boss at a logging camp near the Dungarvon River in New Brunswick, Canada, killed the camp cook to steal his money. He buried the body in the woods some distance from the camp and told the other workers the cook got sick and died. The whooping screams of the dead man's ghost have been heard in the forest near the river ever since—or so they say.

THE WHISTLING GHOST

In Venezuela, the ghost of a tall, thin man is said to roam at night clutching a bag filled with bones. The ghost pauses at people's doorsteps to count his bones, and if you do not stop to listen to him count, someone in your house might die. Called El Silbón, which means "The Whistler" in Spanish, this tormented ghost emits an eerie whistling sound, but it won't help you avoid him. When the whistle sounds close, El Silbón is far away. But when

the whistle sounds very distant, El Silbón is right next to you.

THE STONE-DWELLING GHOST

In the Banks Islands in the Pacific Ocean, people once believed that certain very large stones harbored ghosts. If a person's shadow fell across one of the haunted stones, the ghost would suck out his or her soul and the person would quickly die. The stones were strategically placed near people's houses to protect them from vandals when no one was home.

GOMANTONG CAVES

FRIGHT METER

Cockroaches. Bats. Centipedes. Rats. Each can be pretty scary on its own, but imagine them all together—millions of them—in one place. One very dark place.

The Gomantong Caves, on the island of Borneo in Southeast Asia, house about two million bats. When you enter, you can hear them chirping loudly—and you might gag on the rotten-egg scent of their poop (aka guano). The floors of the caves are covered 10 feet deep in the stuff, but

A roach-covered cave wall.

Sunlight briefly penetrates the huge cave.

even with a flashlight, you can't see it. That's because the carpet of poop is covered by a quivering mass of cockroaches. They feast on the guano and instantly devour the occasional bird or bat that is unlucky enough to fall off the 300-foot-high ceiling into it. The cockroaches are ravenous, but they're not selfish: They share their all-you-can-eat buffet with the giant rats, beetles, and crabs that scuttle through the caves.

Human visitors who come to witness this perfect storm of creepy-crawliness perch on a wooden walkway high above the

cave floor, where they are safe from the rats and roaches. Well, *sort of* safe. If you slip on the slimy boards and reach for the handrail, you might end up grabbing an errant cockroach or shaking hands with one of the three-inch-long centipedes that skitter along the cave walls and eat roaches.

Not quite scary enough for you? Did we mention the walk through the jungle to get to the caves? If you're not wearing long sleeves, leeches from nearby plants will latch on to your skin and settle in for a blood smoothie. As you stroll, take a good look at the trees that surround you. See that long, slender leaf? It's actually a venomous green viper in disguise.

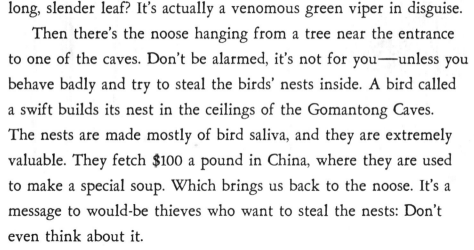

Then there's the noose hanging from a tree near the entrance to one of the caves. Don't be alarmed, it's not for you—unless you behave badly and try to steal the birds' nests inside. A bird called a swift builds its nest in the ceilings of the Gomantong Caves. The nests are made mostly of bird saliva, and they are extremely valuable. They fetch $100 a pound in China, where they are used to make a special soup. Which brings us back to the noose. It's a message to would-be thieves who want to steal the nests: Don't even think about it.

Still not scared? Maybe you are one of the brave souls who should visit the Gomantong Caves. Perhaps you can see the roaches and rats and bats and spiders feeding on one another the way a scientist might: It's a wonderful example of the circle of life in action. On the other hand, you might have this less scientific reaction: *"Ahhhhhhh! Get me out of here!"*

HAUNTED HOUSES

When English billionaire Anwar Rashid bought the house of his dreams in Nottingham, England, in 2007, he thought he and his family would live there for many years. The 52-room mansion had everything a person could want: a movie theater, a gym, 17 bedrooms, and 10 bathrooms. It also had something a person might *not* want. According to Rashid, the old stone house was haunted, and eight months after moving in, the family fled in horror, vowing never to return.

The Rashids said that the first signs the house was haunted appeared the day they moved in. They heard a knocking on the wall and a voice saying, "Is anyone there?" Mr. Rashid looked everywhere but found no one. Minutes later, they heard the voice again. On another occasion, Mrs. Rashid thought she saw one of her daughters watching TV downstairs at 5 a.m. But when she went upstairs to check the daughter's bed, she was sleeping right there. The final straw came when the Rashids found what they believed were drops of blood on their baby son's quilt. They moved out that day.

Was the Rashids' house really haunted? The answer depends on whether or not you believe in paranormal events—experiences that cannot be explained by scientific evidence. People who believe in the paranormal say that a house becomes haunted when ghosts of the dead keep returning. They often make noises, knocking or banging inside the walls, or they produce mysterious smells. Sometimes they are even visible as shadowy figures. Believers in the paranormal say spirits usually haunt a building because something disturbing happened there and they cannot rest in peace.

Those who do not believe in the paranormal say that there is almost always a scientific explanation for things that happen in a supposedly haunted house. Animals can knock things over in the middle of the night, producing weird sounds. The wind or the house itself can create noises (see page 53) and a person's mind can play tricks (see page 54) that make it seem like a house is haunted.

FAMOUS HAUNTED HOUSES

Many houses have a reputation for being haunted. Here are three legendary ones. You'll have to decide for yourself if you think the ghosts said to live in them are real!

A GRISLY MURDER: THE LIZZIE BORDEN HOUSE

On a hot August morning in 1892, a terrible crime took place at the home of Abby and Andrew Borden in Fall River, Massachusetts. Mrs. Borden was making a bed in the guest room when someone crept up behind her and killed her with an ax. Less than two hours later, her husband was murdered in the same grisly fashion. The couple's daughter, Lizzie, was accused of the awful crime, but there was not enough evidence to convict her.

To this day, the double murder remains unsolved—and some say that the ghosts of the Bordens haunt their old house. People have reported hearing a woman crying in the guest room. Others say they have seen the ghost of the Bordens' maid, who said she witnessed the crime. Is she trying to tell the truth about what happened? Still others say they have seen the ghost of Mrs. Borden happily puttering around the house. Is she trying to continue the life that was suddenly cut short?

No one knows if the Borden house is really haunted, but you can try finding out for yourself, as the old house is now an inn. You may not get much sleep there, but you might meet a ghost or two during your stay.

BUILT FOR PROTECTION: THE WINCHESTER MYSTERY HOUSE

Imagine living alone in a 160-room house filled with secret passages, hallways that lead nowhere, and staircases that dead-end at the ceiling. Everywhere you look, there are creepy decorations like spiderwebs carved into the wood and objects arranged in groups of 13. It sounds like a haunted-house theme park, but it's a real house that was built more than 100 years ago in San Jose, California, by a woman named Sarah Winchester.

Mrs. Winchester's husband had made a fortune selling Winchester rifles, and after he died, she visited a psychic to help her contact her husband. The psychic had some upsetting news: She said the spirits of people killed by Winchester rifles were angry and would haunt Mrs. Winchester for the rest of her life unless she started building a house—and never stopped.

Mrs. Winchester bought a six-room house, and for the next 38 years, carpenters worked day and night adding rooms to the building. Some say the dead-end hallways and doors that opened

The dark entrance to the mysterious Winchester mansion.

on to blank walls were meant to trap ghosts. Mrs. Winchester took no chances: She reportedly never slept in the same bedroom two nights in a row to make it harder for spirits to find her.

Construction finally stopped when Mrs. Winchester died (of natural causes) in 1922. By then, the house had 10,000 windows, 2,000 doors, and a reputation for being haunted. Today tourists

Watch your step: Some doors, like the one in the far right of this photograph, may lead to a fatal drop.

A door at the top of the stairs that leads only to a blank wall is a trap for ghosts.

can visit the mansion, called the Winchester Mystery House, and see if any spirits are still trapped inside.

GHOSTLY BATTLES: THE BEAUREGARD-KEYES HOUSE

New Orleans is sometimes called the most haunted city in America. Founded in 1718, the city has endured many catastrophes, from Civil War battles to massive fires to destructive hurricanes. Some people say this explains why so many old houses in New Orleans seem to be haunted: When people die violent deaths, they are more likely to return to Earth as ghosts. The Beauregard-Keyes House is reputedly one such house.

Confederate General Pierre G. T. Beauregard lived in the mansion during the Civil War. Legend has it that more than 100 years later, ghostly soldiers appeared in the main hall of the house and fought a fierce battle. Witnesses claimed they could hear cannon shots and smell blood.

In 1970, the house became a museum. A worker there said she never saw any ghosts doing battle, but she claimed that the ghost of a dog named Lucky haunts its master's bedroom.

HAUNT YOUR OWN HOUSE

FRIGHT METER

The chances are good that your house is not haunted. But that doesn't mean you can't fool your family or friends into thinking it is. Here's how to make it seem like ghosts are regular visitors to your address.

HORRIFYING HOW-TO

ADULT HELP

create ghostly footsteps or knocking

One sign of a haunting is the sound of footsteps or unexpected knocking. With two phones and a little bit of planning, you can create your own ghostly noises.

WHAT YOU NEED

- Two phones, at least one of which should be a smartphone.

Ask your parents if you can borrow theirs if necessary.

WHAT YOU DO

Prepare the haunting

1. With a parent's help, download a free ringtone that sounds like footsteps, knocking, or howling (or any other sound you think is ghostlike) onto the smartphone. Listen to the choices until you find one that sounds convincing. We'll call this phone the "ghost phone."

2. Make sure the "vibrate" function is turned off on the ghost phone, and turn up the volume.

3. Test out your ghost phone before you do the actual haunting. Decide where you want the ghostly sounds to come from. A closet in your sibling's bedroom or in a room where your family hangs out in the evening is a good spot. The idea is to find a place where it will seem like a ghost is inside the wall.

When no one is around, put the ghost phone in that spot. Then use your other phone to call the ghost phone. Listen to see if the ringtone can be heard. You might have to adjust the volume.

Do the haunting

1. A day or two before you start the haunting, mention to your sibling or other family members that you heard that several houses in the area are reportedly haunted. You can say something like, "I heard the house down the street is haunted. The family keeps hearing knocking (or footsteps or howling) in the walls at night but there's nothing there." This will get them in the right frame of mind.

2. When you're ready for the haunting to begin, hide the ghost phone in the spot you selected. Pick a time when

-CONTINUED-

you know your "victim" will be entering the room soon. You can hide it in a sibling's closet just before he or she goes to bed. (Make sure your sibling is old enough to handle a ghost, though!) Or hide it in the living room just before everyone gathers to watch TV.

3. When your "victim" is in the room you're haunting, step outside the room and call the ghost phone with your other phone. Wait a few minutes and call again. Make sure you are nearby so you can hear your victim react. If your victim gets up and says there's a weird noise in the closet, go in with your phone hidden behind your back or in your pocket. Make sure the phone is set to dial the ghost phone

number. Pretend to listen for the sound. You can say, "I don't hear anything" and dial the number as you say it. Then act very freaked out when you hear the sound. You can say, "Oh, boy, this is just what they were talking about! It sounds like our house is haunted, too!" Wait awhile and then say, "I guess it stopped," and leave the room. A minute or two later, call the ghost phone again.

4. Use your judgment about how far to take the haunting. You can keep it going for a few nights, or reveal the "ghost" behind the sounds sooner if you think it's wise.

HORRIFYING HOW-TO

create a mysterious smell

Add a strange scent to your ghost noises to make your house seem even more haunted.

WHAT YOU NEED

- A paper towel
- Perfume
- A small paper or plastic cup or an empty 6- or 8-ounce yogurt cup

WHAT YOU DO

Prepare the haunting

1. Tear the paper towel in half and fold one piece so you have a square about 3 inches across.

2. Spray the folded towel with perfume until it's pretty saturated but not soaking wet.

3. Put it in the cup.

Do the haunting

1. When you hide your ghost phone, hide the cup with the scented paper towel in it at the same time.

2. When your ghost phone starts ringing, look in the hiding place as if you are searching for a ghost. Then say to your victim, "Do you smell something strange? You know, ghosts sometimes produce a smell. This is really creepy. Now we have this weird sound *and* a mysterious smell. I'm getting out of here!"

ISLAND OF THE DOLLS

FRIGHT METER

More than 50 years ago, a man named Don Julian Santana Barrera was living all alone on a small island near Mexico City. Decades before, the island had been populated, but by the 1950s, Barrera was the only remaining resident, and most Mexicans didn't even know he was there.

One day Barrera was walking along one of the island's canals when he noticed a doll floating in the water near a spot where a girl was said to have died many years before. He pulled the doll from the water and hung it from a nearby tree in memory of the girl, who likely had drowned while playing.

For Barrera, the doll was the start of an obsession. He began finding old dolls in rubbish heaps and stringing them from trees all over the island. Later, people who visited the island for the day brought him old dolls. By the 1990s, there were not hundreds, but thousands of tattered dolls peering down from the trees, many missing arms or legs. They gave the island an extremely creepy feeling. People who liked scary attractions started coming over by ferry boat to experience the spine-chilling effects of a forest of mutilated dolls.

Some say Barrera hung the dolls because he was haunted by the dead girl's spirit and the dolls were meant to appease her. Others say the dolls were intended to protect the island from evil, while still others believe the dolls themselves are evil. No one can ask Barrera because he died in 2001—in an eerie twist, his body was found in the canal in the same spot where the girl drowned.

If you dare, you can visit the island yourself and see if you can feel the dolls watching you or, even spookier, if you can hear them whisper to one another. Whatever happens, don't miss the last ferry back to the mainland, or you'll end up spending the night with these toys.

ISLAND OF SNAKES

FRIGHT METER

About 90 miles off the coast of Brazil is Ilha da Queimada Grande, a gorgeous, hilly green island that looks from afar like the perfect secluded vacation spot. But the island is actually mobbed, not with people, but with snakes. An estimated 2,000 to 4,000 two-foot-long, extremely venomous golden lancehead vipers live on the tiny island. That translates to at least one snake per square meter—an area smaller than your bed. The forest floor quivers with the vipers and they slither up and down the trees.

Not surprisingly, the Brazilian government doesn't allow anyone except scientific researchers to visit "Snake Island." But between 1909 and 1920, a few people lived on the viper-infested isle to keep the lighthouse running. According to local legend, the last lighthouse keeper and his family met a gruesome end. One night a bunch of snakes crawled in the window of their house and

bit them. The family fled the cottage and started running through the forest to get to their boat. But vipers hanging out in the trees overhead reached down and bit them, too. Needless to say, they never made it off the island.

How did one island end up overrun by so many snakes? The answer goes back about 11,000 years, when sea levels rose and separated the hilly piece of land from the mainland. The snakes that became stranded on the newly formed island had no predators, and they reproduced quickly. They learned to slither up trees to kill birds, their main prey, with their extremely fast-acting venom. The venom melts the flesh around the bite wound and kills most prey instantly.

While Snake Island is definitely a place to avoid, it's also a place that needs protection. Wildlife poachers, disease, and habitat loss have caused the golden lancehead population to drop in recent years, and the snake is now on the endangered list. That's bad news not just for the snake but for humans: Scientists who visit Snake Island believe the vipers' super-powerful venom can treat heart disease and other illnesses. What doesn't kill you may save your life!

JELLYFISH

FRIGHT METER

Jellyfish are gloppy, translucent carnivores that have no brain, no bones, no blood, and no heart. But watch out! When you touch one, tiny but extremely painful stingers called nematocysts rub off on your skin and release venom into your body. Jellyfish don't go out of their way to attack humans, but here are a few you should definitely avoid.

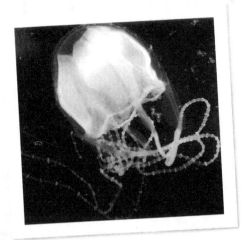

SMALL BUT DEADLY

The Irukandji jellyfish lives in the waters around northern Australia and Florida. Its tentacles are only a couple of feet long at the most, but its venom is far more powerful than that of a cobra. One sting can kill a human. If you survive a sting, you have Irukandji syndrome to look forward to: It causes body pain, nausea, and a feeling of impending doom.

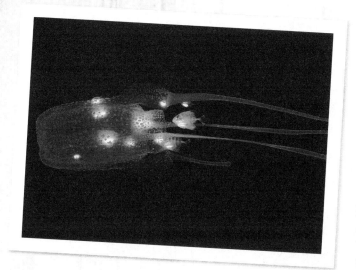

A BIG BOX O' JELLY

On the danger-o-meter, the box jellyfish takes the top spot. It's found off the northern coast of Australia and is a relative of the Irukandji, but it grows to be much bigger. Its tentacles can span more than 10 feet. But it's what's *on* the tentacles that's really scary: Each one contains about 5,000 stinging cells that inject deadly venom. A single sting can bring a person down in seconds, as the venom attacks the heart, nervous system, and skin. One box jellyfish can hold enough venom in its tentacles to kill 60 people.

While the sting of a box jellyfish can kill anything from a fish to a person, the box turtle is immune to its effects and actually hunts the tentacled invertebrate.

The lion's mane jellyfish has around 800 tentacles that can grow up to more than 100 feet long.

Most jellyfish do not have brains, but this one does—four, in fact. And it's got 24 eyes to track its victims. While most jellyfish drift along wherever the ocean current takes them, the

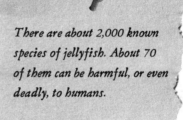

There are about 2,000 known species of jellyfish. About 70 of them can be harmful, or even deadly, to humans.

box jellyfish can propel itself through the water at speeds of up to five miles per hour by repeatedly contracting its bell-like body (known as its umbrella).

ROAR! THE LION'S MANE JELLYFISH

The largest of all jellyfish is the lion's mane jellyfish. It has up to 800 tentacles that, together, look like a gigantic lion's mane. One of the largest ones ever recorded had tentacles that were 120 feet long and a main body that was eight feet wide. From tentacle tip to tentacle tip, this jellyfish measured about the same as the width of a soccer field.

A sting from a lion's mane jellyfish, which lives in the Arctic Ocean, northern Atlantic Ocean, and northern Pacific Ocean, is not as deadly as one from the box jellyfish, but it can cause some serious harm. Hey, just the sight of one might scare you to death.

KILLER BEES

FRIGHT METER

Most bees are not out to get you. They just want to be left alone to mind their own business, which is pollinating plants. But there's one kind of bee that you *should* be afraid of. Its name alone is scary: the killer bee.

These very aggressive stingers came into being when a lab experiment went bad back in the mid-1950s. Entomologists (scientists who study insects) were looking for a way to increase honey production. They sent some African honeybees to Brazil, planning to crossbreed them with local bees to create super honey-producers. A year later, several swarms of the African bees escaped from the experimental hives and started to mate with local honeybees. As a result, a new type of bee was born: Africanized honeybees, also known as killer bees.

Killer bees *look* like the European honeybees we're familiar

with (they're a tiny bit smaller), and their venom is not any more powerful. What makes them more dangerous is that they are much easier to disturb. When they get upset, they swarm in large groups that for unknown reasons sometimes land on people. If the person gets agitated (and who wouldn't get agitated if 40,000 bees landed on their arm?), the bees get agitated, too. That's when they start to sting. To make things worse, their stings give off a scent similar to that of bananas, which attracts other bees, which then makes the killer bees even angrier. One more scary behavior: Killer bees have been known to chase a target (yes, that includes a human target) for as far as a quarter mile if they feel threatened. And they're fast.

Beware: When Africanized honeybees, aka killer bees, get upset, they react 10 times faster than European honeybees.

COMING TO AMERICA

In 1990, killer bees made it north to the United States, showing up in Texas and Arizona. Three years later, a man in Texas became the first person in the United States to die from killer bee stings after he tried to remove a hive. Since then, they have spread to more states in the South and the West.

Death by killer bee is relatively rare in the United States, but an estimated 1,000 people worldwide have died from their stings since the 1950s. Often, these are people who cannot outrun the bees and end up dying from a massive number of stings.

While this is all scary enough to send you into your own hive forever, the most serious threat from killer bees isn't the "killer" part, it's what they do to other bees. When Africanized bees move into an area, they often push out the native bee species,

threatening their survival which, in turn, threatens the health of that area's entire ecosystem.

CREEPY CREATURES

KOMODO DRAGON

FRIGHT METER

"Giant flesh-eating lizard attacks human!" It sounds like the tagline for a horror movie. But it's an accurate description of an animal that really exists: the Komodo dragon.

This aptly named creature looks like a cross between a dragon and a dinosaur, with its long, flat head, scaly skin, forked tongue, and enormous, muscular tail. As lizards go, it's definitely a giant: The Komodo dragon can grow to be 10 feet long and weigh more than 200 pounds. And it has an appetite to match. When this fearsome predator gets hungry, it's time to get lost. It will eat just about anything that's made of flesh, including deer, pigs, giant water buffalo, and yes, humans, although that doesn't happen too often. And its table manners are what you might describe as "vicious."

Komodo dragons live on islands off the coast of Indonesia, not far from Australia, where their grayish-brown skin provides

excellent camouflage for hiding in wait for prey. The lizard uses its long yellow tongue to smell and can pick up an animal's scent from up to four miles away. It waits patiently for its prey to walk by, then leaps out, knocks the animal to the ground, and tears it to pieces with its long, curved claws and its large teeth, which are serrated like a shark's. Sometimes the Komodo dragon shakes its victim to break its neck if the claws and teeth aren't doing the trick. Conveniently, the lizard cannot hear high-pitched sounds, so a victim's shrieks or howls fall on deaf ears.

If an animal manages to narrowly escape with only a bite wound, it doesn't usually live for long. Komodo dragon saliva contains venom that will kill an animal within a day or two. Since Komodo dragons don't like to waste food, they will sniff out the carcass and enjoy a day-old feast.

These fellows love to eat so

REASONS TO LOVE KOMODO DRAGONS

While Komodo dragons may seem like the most awful animals on Earth, they actually need protection because loss of habitat is threatening their survival. And these giant lizards have some very appealing qualities (as long as they are not attacking you). They are easy to tame and bond well with humans. Many zookeepers say they are the most intelligent reptiles in the world. Just don't make them mad.

much that they will even dine on their own kind. Adult Komodo dragons are known to gobble up young dragons that make the mistake of coming down from the trees where they spend most of their time.

To stay safe on the ground, juveniles sometimes pull a rather ingenious—and, to humans, disgusting—trick. When an adult Komodo dragon makes a kill, it eats just about every part of the animal, including the intestines. To empty out any feces in the intestines, the dragon swings the organs around over its head until the poop flies out. Young dragons then roll around in the stuff to make themselves unappetizing to the adult dragons. Smelling bad is a small price to pay for getting to live.

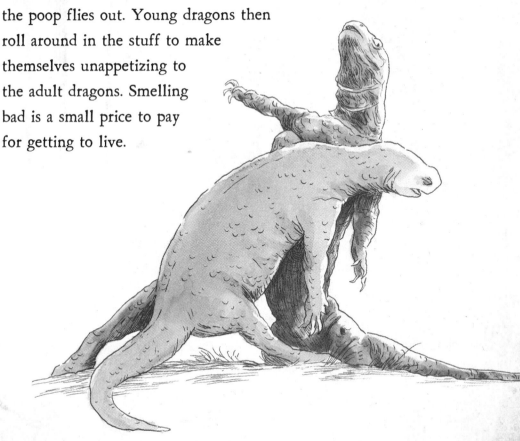

LAKE NATRON: PETRIFYING WATERS

FRIGHT METER

Imagine coming upon a shimmering lake after walking for hours through dry, cracked land on a boiling-hot day. You wade into the water, hoping to cool off, but almost instantly your body seems to turn to stone. You cannot move or breathe. You have been

petrified—literally—your body dried out and hardened, and you are doomed to remain as a lifelike statue on the shores of the lake for eternity.

It sounds like something out of a fairy tale, but it's exactly what happens to unlucky animals that enter the deadly waters of Lake Natron in Tanzania, Africa. The lake is loaded with a saltlike chemical compound called natron, which forms naturally from the volcanic ash that surrounds the lake. The compound doesn't just kill creatures that enter the lake; it makes their tissues calcify, or harden, as they dry. To make things even more grisly, the lake is usually bloodred from bacteria that live there, and the temperature can reach a scalding 120° Fahrenheit.

Photographer Nick Brandt visited the lake in 2012 and found the perfectly preserved bodies of bats and birds that had tried to cross the 30-mile-long lake and had fallen in. The bodies washed up on the shore when water levels receded during the dry season. With an eye for art, Brandt arranged the birds on the lake and photographed them, giving them eerie new life in pictures.

PETRIFYING PLANTS

MANCHINEEL TREE

FRIGHT METER
1 2 3

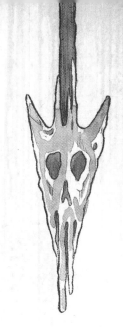

With its shiny green leaves and delicious-looking fruit, the manchineel tree seems like the perfect place to seek shelter from the hot sun. But this tree, which grows on the beaches of southern Florida, the Caribbean, and Central America, is not your friend. It has been called the most dangerous tree in the world. Moments after you bite into the plum-flavored fruit, nicknamed "little apples of death" by the Spanish, your mouth starts to burn so badly it feels like the skin is being ripped open. Soon your throat swells so much it closes up, making it extremely painful to eat or drink.

In Central America, the manchineel tree provides a home to an iguana that is immune to its poison.

The fruit is plenty scary—but it isn't even the worst part of this tree. A poisonous white sap oozes out of the manchineel's twigs, leaves, and bark that can give you blisters so bad you end up in the hospital. And if you are ever tempted to burn manchineel wood for a beach campfire, don't: The smoke can cause temporary or even permanent blindness.

Hundreds of years ago, Indians living in Florida dipped their arrows in manchineel sap to make them poisonous—which at least provided a quicker death than eating the fruits.

Above: A "death apple," the small green fruit that grows on the toxic manchineel tree. Right: A sign warning visitors.

MONSTERS

FRIGHT METER

Wherever there are people, there are monsters. Maybe it's because monsters like scaring people. Or maybe it's because monsters need people to dream them up. We've collected some of the most horrid legendary monsters from around the world. Which one would you most hate to find in your closet?

The Latin root of the word monster is the verb monere, which means "to warn."

CERBERUS

This three-headed dog with a serpent's tail, a mane of snakes, and a lion's claws guards the entrance to Hades, the ancient Greek underworld. Cerberus is quick to attack, but you might get around this hellhound by distracting him with a piece of honey cake.

LA MANO PELUDA

La Mano Peluda means "hairy hand" in Spanish, and that's exactly what this monster is: a severed hand that's covered with hair. Some say the hand belongs to a man who was murdered more than 400 years ago during the bloody Spanish Inquisition. La Mano Peluda gets revenge by grabbing people, especially young children, by the feet at night while they are sleeping.

MEDUSA

In Greek mythology, the goddess Athena curses the beautiful Medusa and transforms her into a hideous, withered, ancient-looking woman with deadly snakes instead of hair. Anyone who meets Medusa's gaze immediately turns to stone.

THE KRAKEN

Running into a regular octopus would be scary enough, but imagine encountering an island-size version of such a sea creature. The legendary Kraken from Norse folklore rises up from under the water to reveal huge horns that can destroy a ship. The Kraken doesn't *want* to hurt anyone. It is just so big—up to a mile long, according to some accounts—that it destroys anything around it when it comes up looking for food.

THE LOCH NESS MONSTER

The Loch Ness Monster is one of the best-known monsters in the world. For 1,500 years, people have speculated that there was something strange in Scotland's

deep and murky Loch Ness. Modern "sightings" of a large, dinosaur-shaped creature were first reported in the 1930s, and since then, people have claimed to see "Nessie" rear her huge head every few years.

CĂPCĂUN

The word *căpcăun* probably once meant "dog head" in Romanian, and this monster from Romanian

folklore is an evil ogre with a dog's head. Sometimes it has four eyes: two on its face and two on the back of its neck. Like certain witches, this monster likes to kidnap children and eat them for dinner.

MONGOLIAN DEATH WORM

This enormous red worm haunts the Gobi Desert of Mongolia. It can stretch as long as five feet and it resembles a cow's intestine (trust us, that's scary). If that's not enough to make you run, consider this: When you come near it, the death worm spits acid that will kill you instantly.

MAPINGUARY

Believed by many to inhabit the Amazon rain forest, the mapinguary (or mapinguari) has been described as a slothlike creature with one or two eyes, and sometimes, a mouth in its stomach. Legend has it that the

mapinguary keeps an eye—or two—out for people who kill more plants and animals than they need to survive. Some scientists believe the mapinguary is actually a rarely seen giant sloth, but that doesn't explain the horrible smell this creature is said to emit. If you see one coming, hold your nose and run as fast as you can!

TIKOLOSHE

This evil-spirited gremlin appears in myths of the Zulu people of South Africa. The short, hairy, human-looking creature is sometimes described as having only one butt cheek, which could make sitting down a challenge. It can make itself

invisible by swallowing a pebble—the better to sneak up on you and scare you or, if it's really in a bad mood, kill you.

EL CHUPACABRA

Some say this creature is hairless, with lizardlike qualities. Some say it has red eyes and can hypnotize and paralyze victims just by looking at them. And others claim it has long fangs to drain the blood from goats and other farm animals—*chupacabra* means "goat sucker" in Spanish. Nonbelievers argue that it's probably just a type of hairless

Mexican dog called a *xoloitzcuintle*. Whether monster or pooch, the first sighting of El Chupacabra was reported in the 1990s. Since then, people in Mexico, Central and South America, Puerto Rico, and the United States claim to have seen it.

BASILISCO CHILOTE

This hybrid monster has the body of a snake and the head and feathers of a rooster. It lives on Chiloé Island in Chile, where it digs holes under people's houses and then secretly drinks their spit until they die of dehydration.

The only way to kill Basilisco Chilote if it invades your home is to burn down the entire house.

PLAT-EYE

This monster from West Indian folklore is a huge black dog with enormous glowing eyes the size of plates (as its name hints). The dog sometimes appears on an isolated road seeking to avenge a wrongful death. In some stories, the unfortunate person who meets up with the beast can see only its fiery eyes, which grow larger and larger until they swallow up the victim.

JERSEY DEVIL

This bizarre horse-headed bat-dragon has gigantic wings, oversized hooves, huge teeth, and according to some, a set of sharp horns. Legend has it that a baby born in the 1700s sprouted wings and turned into a violent, merciless creature known to slaughter pets and cattle and climb onto people's roofs. It's lived deep in New Jersey's wooded Pine Barrens for nearly 300 years.

YARA-MA-YHA-WHO

This hideous, short, red-skinned humanoid appears in the myths of Australia's aboriginal people. It has no teeth, but that doesn't prevent it from sucking your blood. The yara-ma-yha-who waits in a tree for a victim to walk by. Then it jumps down and uses the suckers on its hands and feet to drink the person's blood. Sometimes it will eat an entire human, but that doesn't necessarily mean certain death: After a nap, the yara-ma-yha-who may vomit the meal back up and the victim might still be alive. This gruesome process may occur repeatedly. If it happens too many times, though, the human turns into a yara-ma-yha-who.

KAPPA

Some say this water demon is part duck, part frog, and part turtle, while

others compare it to a child-sized salamander with a semihuman appearance. Either way, the kappa is green, spends most of its time in the water, and loves cucumbers. It also loves to drown people by pulling them underwater. Parents have been known to use this legendary monster from Japanese folklore to scare kids into being careful when they go swimming. It has an indentation on its head, where a small puddle of liquid helps it maintain its powers, because a dried-up kappa is a useless kappa.

SASQUATCH

This creature is said to look like a cross between a gorilla and a human. It stands seven to nine feet tall, is covered with hair, and has an awful odor. Some people call it Bigfoot because of the large footprints they claim it has left behind as it roams through Canada and the Pacific Northwest U.S.

CRYPTID CORNER

Many of the monsters on these pages could be classified as cryptids—animals that people claim to have seen, but whose existence has never been scientifically proven. The cloud of mystery surrounding many of these bizarre creatures is enough to keep some people wondering—and searching.

VETALA

Invisible demons from Hindu mythology, vetala inhabit corpses at burial grounds or crematoriums. They transform the corpses into vampires and then get going on their ultimate goals: killing some people— especially children—and driving others to insanity. If the vetala's host body gets destroyed, the vetala just moves on to another host and gets back to business.

MUJINA

FRIGHT METER

This ghost story takes place in Japan and features a phantom the writer calls a mujina. *It is not a violent or gory tale, but may leave you feeling quietly horrified. This version is adapted from a book of Japanese ghost stories collected by the 19th-century Irish writer Lafcadio Hearn.*

One late night, a merchant was hurrying home along a very dark, deserted street in Tokyo (this was long before there were streetlights). He noticed a young woman, all alone, crouching at the edge of a nearby canal. She was sobbing bitterly. Worried that she intended to drown herself, the merchant rushed over to try to help her. As he got close, he noticed that she was small and graceful and beautifully dressed. She had her hair done like someone from a wealthy family.

"Miss, please do not cry like that!" the merchant said, trying to console her. "What is wrong? Tell me how I can help you, and I will do anything you ask." The merchant meant what he said. He was a very kind man.

But the woman kept on sobbing, hiding her face from him with one of her long sleeves. "Miss," he said again, as gently as he could. "Please, please listen to me! This is no place for a young lady at night! Do not cry, please! Only tell me how I may be of some help to you!"

Slowly she stood up, but turned her back to him, and

continued to moan and sob behind her sleeve. The merchant touched her shoulder gently and pleaded: "Miss! Miss! Listen to me, just for one little moment! Miss!"

It was then that the woman turned to him and dropped her sleeve. She stroked her face with her hand, and the man saw that she had no eyes or nose or mouth. Her face was as smooth as an egg. He screamed in horror and ran up the street into the pitch-black night. He ran and ran and ran. All was black and empty before him. He kept running, never daring to look back. At last he saw a lantern, so far away that it looked like the gleam of a firefly; he ran for it. He was desperate to talk to someone. As he got closer, he saw that it was the light of a noodle vendor. He flung himself at the noodle seller, crying out, "*Aa!—aa!!—aa!!!*"

"What happened?" exclaimed the noodle seller. "Did someone hurt you?"

"No—nobody hurt me," panted the merchant, "only . . . *Aa!—aa!*" He could barely speak.

"Only scared you?" asked the vendor. "Was it robbers?"

"Not robbers, not robbers," gasped the terrified man. "I saw . . . I saw a woman—by the canal; and she showed me . . . *Aa!* I cannot tell you what she showed me!"

"Oh? Was it anything like this?" asked the noodle man. The merchant stared as the noodle man stroked his own face and his features disappeared. His face was as smooth as an egg. And at that moment, the light went out.

MUMMIES

FRIGHT METER

Imagine being all alone in a cobwebbed tomb with an ancient Egyptian mummy. You're so close you can touch the leathery skin, see every scraggly hair on the scalp, every fingernail on the 2,000-year-old hands, and smell the musty odor. Alarming thoughts flit through your mind. Could the mummy leap out of its coffin and grab you? It's just a dead body, you tell yourself. Just a very old, very dead body . . . that's making you *very* afraid.

For the ancient Egyptians, there was nothing scary about a preserved corpse. It was needed to carry a person's soul to the afterlife. Most of us, however, aren't as comfortable with death— or with mummies—as the Egyptians were. It's hard not to think they might come to life when we're not looking. Or put a curse on us!

Archaeologist Howard Carter and an assistant inspecting Tut's tomb and, according to legend, unleashing the curse.

THE MUMMY'S CURSE

In November 1922, after years of digging around in Egypt, British archaeologist Howard Carter finally uncovered the tomb of the pharaoh Tutankhamen, aka King Tut, in the Valley of the Kings. Newspapers in Britain went crazy reporting on the mummy and the treasures found inside his tomb, but the most riveting stories were about the curse supposedly inscribed on the wall of Tut's burial chamber: "Death shall come on swift wings to him that toucheth the tomb of Pharaoh."

According to newspaper reports, it didn't take long for the curse to go into effect. On the very day Carter entered the tomb, a cobra, the symbol of Egyptian kings, killed his pet canary. About six weeks later, Lord Carnarvon, the man who paid for the expedition, suddenly died from a mosquito bite. Later, Carter's friend's house burned down—not once, but twice. The friend had reportedly received a gift from the archaeologist, a paperweight made of a mummified hand wearing a bracelet

A French newspaper reports on the discovery.

with the message: "Cursed be he who moves my body." Then there were more deaths. Newspapers reported that by 1935, 21 members of Carter's team had died.

Was the Mummy's Curse real? The evidence seemed convincing at the time, but most of it was invented by reporters or easily explained by natural events. Still, like a mummy's soul, the idea of a curse never dies. In 2013, a British newspaper reported that a small statue found in an Egyptian tomb had started spinning by itself inside its museum case. Some say vibrations from visitors' footsteps caused the spinning. Or was it the Return of the Mummy's Curse?

MEET SOME REAL MUMMIES

Egyptian mummies may be the most famous, but they aren't the only ones in the world. In fact, mummies have been found on every continent. What they all have in common is that they still have some skin clinging to their old, dried-out bones—and sometimes muscles and organs, too. And all can look pretty scary.

BOG MAN

On a spring day in 1950, a family in Denmark was digging for peat, a rich soil that is often burned to heat builings, when they found themselves staring at the body of a man with leathery skin and a noose around his neck. Thinking they had stumbled upon a recent crime victim, they called the police. Little did they know that the man had been murdered 2,400 years before. His killers dumped the body in what was then a marsh.

Over the centuries, the marsh dried out and formed a peat bog, which has the perfect conditions for mummifying a body: The bacteria that would normally make a corpse decay cannot survive there, and the plants help preserve flesh. Tollund Man, as the murder victim is called, is

Tollund Man's body is evidence of a nearly 2,500-year-old crime.

so well preserved that you can see the pores in his skin and the beard stubble on his face.

STILL SMILING AFTER ALL THESE YEARS

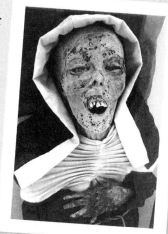

In 1994, a worker in the town of Vác, Hungary, was checking the walls of an old church for cracks when he found something much more interesting—or terrifying, depending how you feel about dead bodies. When the worker tapped a brick wall, it crumbled to reveal a stone staircase that led to a huge room stacked floor to ceiling with coffins. When anthropologists looked inside the coffins, they found themselves eye to eye with 265 amazingly well-preserved mummies, staring up as if they'd been patiently waiting 200 years for this moment. The mummies' clothes were in near-perfect condition and their skin was intact, even if their faces had caved in a bit.

When the church crypt was sealed in 1838, no one realized that conditions were perfect for natural mummification: Cool, dry air and oil from the pinewood coffins prevented decay.

These lifelike mummies may end up helping people who are still alive today: Most of them had tuberculosis, or the White Plague, as the disease was called when it ravaged Europe in the 1700s and 1800s. Scientists are studying tissue samples from the mummies to find out how some people resisted the disease.

A MUMMY TO *DAI* FOR

Many mummies have been found in the desert areas of China where the dry, salty air preserved flesh (much like a piece of dried fruit). One of the most lifelike mummies ever found is a 50-year-old Chinese noblewoman known as Lady Dai. When she died more than 2,000 years ago, she was buried in a series of nesting coffins that were then covered with several tons of charcoal. The charcoal absorbed any moisture that might have seeped into the coffin and allowed bacteria to decompose the flesh. As a result, Lady Dai is so well preserved, it's as though she had died just moments ago. Her skin is still soft to the touch, there is blood in her veins, and

her brain and other organs are whole. Scientists who examined her were able to count 138 melon seeds in her stomach!

A MUMMY TO WATCH OVER THEM

The Egyptians buried their mummies in sealed tombs, wished them safe travels to the afterlife, and never saw them again. But in some cultures, people show respect for the dead by keeping

A mummified Anga chief watches over his village.

their mummified bodies close by and involving them in daily life.

For centuries, the Anga (or Agnu) people of Papua

SCREAMING MUMMIES

Why do so many mummies look like they're screaming in agony? Muscles connected to the skull keep your mouth shut when you're alive, but once you die, the muscles relax and your jawbone naturally hangs open, which can make it look like you're screaming for help. In Victorian times, chin straps or handkerchiefs were used to hold a corpse's jaw closed. The ancient Egyptians also tried keeping mummies' jaws shut, but it didn't always work. Or were some mummies not as dead as they looked?

New Guinea mummified their loved ones using a smoking process much like curing meat. Mummified chiefs would be placed on chairs on a cliff high above the village where they could continue to watch over everyone. Every so often, villagers would bring a mummified leader down to participate in community activities.

In the 1950s, Christian missionaries put a stop to the tradition, though the Anga are working to bring it back.

MODERN MUMMIES

Most mummies show some wear and tear over the years—their skin sags, their bones stick out, what little hair they have is a mess. But in the last century, a few famous political leaders have been mummified using newer technology, and the results are frighteningly lifelike.

Russian leader Vladimir Lenin died just two years after the discovery of King Tut's tomb, which inspired the Russians to preserve his body. Scientists developed a secret process that requires regular bathing in preservative chemicals. You can still view Lenin (when he is not taking a bath) in a mausoleum in Moscow.

Not to be outdone, the Chinese mummified their leader Mao Zedong's body in 1976, and hundreds of thousands of people view it every year.

The mummy of Chinese leader Mao Zedong.

NEPENTHES, THE FLESH-EATING PLANT

Most plants feed themselves by quietly converting sunlight into food. But a few plants have a more sinister appetite: They like to eat flesh. *Live* flesh. The Venus flytrap is the most famous, but there's another, even creepier family of carnivorous plants called *Nepenthes*, also known as pitcher plants.

Nepenthes plants grow in Southeast Asia and Australia and have large pitcher- or cup-shaped flowers that lure insects with their sweet-smelling nectar. The cups also attract larger prey, including mice, rats, lizards, and even birds.

When insects or larger prey arrive to feast, they try to perch on a pitcher plant's slippery rim, but quickly lose their footing. They slide down the waxy walls of the cup into a pool of water and struggle not to drown. But drowning might be preferable to what happens next. The plant starts to produce a powerful digestive acid that slowly dissolves the creature's flesh. The largest pitcher plants can produce as much as two quarts of deadly acid—enough to drown a fully grown rat.

Some varieties of Nepenthes are even more gruesome. One has a chamber in the stem where ants live. When hunger strikes, they march down to the death pit, grab a piece of decaying flesh, and carry it up to the top, where they have a picnic. What they don't eat drops back down to the pit, where it decays much faster. Of course, decaying flesh is good for the plant, but bad news for anyone who walks by. Visitors to a botanic garden in France once complained about a disgusting smell. Workers found a partially digested mouse inside a large Nepenthes.

THE OPEN WINDOW

FRIGHT METER

In this story, one of the characters is playing a trick that involves ghosts. See if you can figure out what the trick is before you get to the end. The version here is adapted from the original, written by the British author H. H. Munro, under the pen name Saki.

"My aunt will be down soon, Mr. Nuttel," said a very self-possessed young girl of 15. "In the meantime you must try and put up with me."

Framton Nuttel tried to say the right thing. Privately he doubted whether visiting these total strangers would do much toward helping the anti-anxiety treatment that he was supposed to be undergoing.

"I know how it will be," his sister had said when he was preparing to leave for this retreat in the country. "You will not speak to a living soul, and your nerves will be worse than ever from moping. I shall just give you letters of introduction to all the people I know there. Some of them, as far as I can remember, were quite nice."

Framton wondered whether Mrs. Sappleton, the self-possessed girl's aunt, was one of the nice ones.

"Do you know many of the people 'round here?" asked the niece after a while.

"Hardly a soul," said Framton. "My sister was staying here, you know, some four years ago, and she gave me letters of introduction to some of the people here."

"Then you know practically nothing about my aunt?" she said.

"Only her name and address," admitted Framton. He was wondering whether Mrs. Sappleton was married or widowed. Something about the room seemed to suggest a man lived there, too.

"Her great tragedy happened just three years ago," said the niece. "That would be since your sister's time here."

"Her tragedy?" asked Framton. Somehow in this restful country spot tragedies seemed out of place.

"You may wonder why we keep that window wide open on an October afternoon," said the niece, pointing to a large French window that opened onto a lawn.

"It is quite warm for the time of the year," said Framton. "But has that window got anything to do with the tragedy?"

"Out through that window, three years ago today, her husband and her two young brothers went off for their day's hunting. They never came back. In crossing the field to their favorite hunting ground they were all three swallowed up in a treacherous piece of marshy wetland. It had been that dreadful wet summer, you know, and places that were safe in other years gave way suddenly without warning. Their bodies were never recovered. That was the dreadful part of it." Here the niece's voice lost its self-possessed note and started to waver. "Poor Aunt always thinks that they will come back someday, they and the little brown spaniel that was lost with them, and walk in at that window just as they used to do. That is why the window is kept open every evening till dusk. Poor dear Aunt, she has often told me how they went out, her husband with his white waterproof coat over his arm, and Ronnie, her youngest brother, singing 'Bertie, why do you bound?' as he always did to tease her, because she said it got on her nerves. Do you know, sometimes on still, quiet evenings like this, I almost get a creepy feeling that they will all walk in through that window——"

She broke off with a little shudder. It was a relief to Framton when the aunt bustled into the room with a whirl of apologies for being late.

"I hope Vera has been amusing you?" she said.

"She has been very interesting," said Framton.

"I hope you don't mind the open window," said Mrs. Sappleton briskly. "My husband and brothers will be home directly from shooting, and they always come in this way. They've been out hunting in the marshes today, so they'll make a fine mess over my poor carpets."

She rattled on cheerfully about her husband and brothers. To Framton it was all purely horrible. He tried to turn the conversation to a less ghastly topic; he noticed that his hostess was giving him only half of her attention, and her eyes were constantly straying past him to the open window and the lawn beyond. It was certainly an unfortunate coincidence that he should have paid his visit on this tragic anniversary.

"The doctors agree in ordering me complete rest, an absence of mental excitement, and avoidance of anything in the nature of violent physical exercise," announced Framton, trying desperately to change the subject.

"Oh?" said Mrs. Sappleton, in a voice that only replaced a yawn at the last moment. Then she suddenly brightened into alert attention—but not to what Framton was saying.

"Here they are at last!" she cried. "Just in time for tea, and don't they look as if they were muddy up to the eyes!"

Framton shivered slightly and turned toward the niece with a look intended to show sympathy for the aunt's sad condition. But she was staring out through the open window with dazed horror in her eyes. In a chill shock of nameless fear Framton swung around in his seat and looked in the same direction.

In the deepening twilight three figures were walking across the lawn toward the window; they all carried guns under their arms, and one of them had a white coat hung over his shoulders. A tired brown spaniel kept close at their heels. Noiselessly they neared the house, and then a hoarse young voice chanted out of the dusk: "I said, Bertie, why do you bound?"

Framton grabbed wildly at his walking stick and hat. He barely noticed the hall door, the gravel drive, and the front gate as he ran headlong out of the house. A cyclist coming along the road had to run into the hedge to avoid a collision.

"Here we are, my dear," said Mr. Sappleton, coming in through the window. "We're fairly muddy, but most of it's dry. Who was that who bolted out as we came up?"

"A most extraordinary man, a Mr. Nuttel," said Mrs. Sappleton. "He could only talk about his illnesses, and dashed off without a word of good-bye or apology when you arrived. One would think he had seen a ghost."

"I expect it was the spaniel," said the niece calmly. "He told me he had a fear of dogs. He was once hunted into a cemetery somewhere on the banks of the Ganges River in India by a pack of dogs, and had to spend the night in a newly dug grave with the creatures snarling and grinning and foaming just above him. Enough to make anyone lose their nerve."

Invention at short notice was her specialty.

OUIJA BOARD

The 1800s were a good time to be a ghost in Europe and America. Many people were obsessed with communicating with the dead. Some hired mediums, people who claimed they could receive messages from spirits, to help them. And some mediums got "help" from a special table that had the letters A to Z, the numbers 0 to 9, and simple words like "yes" or "no" painted on top. Mediums would place their fingers on a small rod with pointed ends that rested on the table and ask a question. Then they would wait for the spirit to guide the pointer from letter to letter to spell out the answer.

Some said the table was a hoax, but the public was fascinated by the idea that they could receive instant messages from "beyond." In the 1880s, people started making their own board-sized versions of the table to use at home. Two people would place their hands on a tiny four-legged table with a pointer, ask a question, and wait for the pointer to move around the board, stopping on certain words or letters.

Soon three savvy businessmen got the idea to make a game based on the popular talking boards. The story goes that they named their game the "Ouija" board because the board spelled out *OUIJA* when they asked what they should call it. In 1891, Ouija boards went on sale, and the public snapped up the "magical" device that promised to answer questions about the "past, present, and future with marvelous accuracy."

Newspapers reported on some creepy effects Ouija boards had on people. In 1916, a woman named Pearl Curran began writing stories and poems that she said were dictated to her through a Ouija board by the spirit of a 17th-century Englishwoman. Curran ended up becoming a publishing success. In 1978, professors at a university in Italy asked a Ouija board to tell them the location of a politician who had been kidnapped. The board spelled out "Gradoli." Later, police discovered that the politician had been held in a house on a street called Via Gradoli.

Do Ouija boards really let you receive messages from spirits? Scientists say it *seems* like an outside force is moving your hand from letter to letter, but in fact, your hand muscles are responding to what your eyes and mind are doing. When you look at a particular letter, your hand will follow in that direction. Others say it really is a spirit from beyond sending a message. Of course, you can always ask the board itself!

PARIS CATACOMBS

FRIGHT METER

Visitors to Paris who are feeling brave head for the Catacombs, a network of tunnels that lie five stories beneath the city streets. The dank, pitch-black corridors are enough to scare most people. But what makes the Catacombs supremely creepy is what's on the walls and ceilings: Every inch is covered with human bones and skulls from over five million skeletons. It's enough to make you wish you'd visited the Eiffel Tower instead.

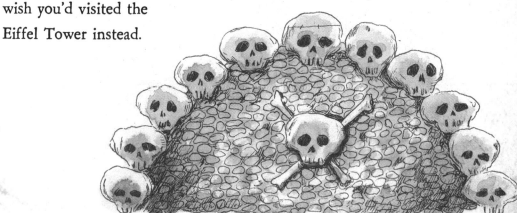

NO ROOM AT THE CEMETERY

The Catacombs were created hundreds of years ago to address a serious—or should we say *grave*—problem. In the 1700s, the population of Paris was booming, and after nearly 1,000 years of use, the cemetery for the poor, Les Innocents, was full. Actually, it was more than full—it was overflowing. Parisians complained about the stench of half-buried corpses, and people who lived nearby were getting sick.

City officials decided to close the cemetery but they needed a place to move all the bones. They decided to use the miles of empty tunnels under the city that were left over from quarries that supplied the stone to build Paris. The transfer would take more than 50 years.

At first, the bones were dumped in piles inside the tunnel. But in 1810, an official decided to transform the tunnels into a macabre work of art. He arranged thousands of skulls and bones in neat rows along the walls and ceilings. The last bones were placed in the Catacombs in 1859.

In the early 1800s, the Catacombs opened to the public, and today you can take a tour of a one-mile bone-filled stretch of the 186-mile network of tunnels. There are unofficial entrances all over the city, but we don't recommend exploring the tunnels on your own. In 2011, three people got lost for two days in the giant labyrinth, which is so deep underground that cell phones don't work. Luckily, the trio left behind notes as they searched for an exit, and one of the notes helped the police find them.

QUICKSAND

FRIGHT METER

A woman is standing on a beautiful Caribbean beach watching the sun set when all of a sudden, she feels her feet being pulled down into the sand. She tries to lift one foot, but it only makes the other foot sink deeper. Suddenly she realizes what is happening: She is standing in quicksand. It grips her feet like freshly poured concrete, and she cannot move. The tide is coming in, and if she doesn't get help soon, she could drown. She starts to scream, but when the rescuers finally get to her, it's too late.

Quicksand sounds like the stuff of horror movies, but it's real, and if you step in it, it can trap you. Here's how it works: Quicksand is a mixture of sand, water, clay, and some salt that forms naturally near coastal areas, lakes, underground springs, and swamps when water seeps into sandy soil. The loosely packed grains of sand are held together by gel-like clay. When an unlucky person steps on the stuff, the sudden force turns the gel-like clay to liquid. That's when the trouble starts. The grains of sand suddenly clump together—tightly—and they end up squeezing onto the victim's feet and legs. The grip is so strong that pulling someone out of quicksand requires the amount of force needed to lift a car.

WHY IT'S CALLED "QUICKSAND"

You might think quicksand got its name because the stuff traps you in a hurry, but centuries ago, the word *quick* meant "living" and *quicksand* means "living sand." It makes sense if you think about the way quicksand moves and then grabs onto you when you step in it. It's as if it is alive.

In the movie version of quicksand, victims get sucked in until their head sinks below the surface and they can't breathe. In fact, the human body floats in quicksand, so while you can get stuck up to your ankles or waist, you won't suffocate. The real danger is getting trapped on the beach of a river or ocean at low tide. If you don't get out in time, you could end up drowning.

HOW TO ESCAPE FROM QUICKSAND

It doesn't happen often, but if the idea of getting trapped in quicksand makes you nervous, read these tips on how to free yourself.

- Do not ask your friends to pull you out. They'll end up yanking you "into two pieces," says physics professor Dr. Daniel Bonn, who has studied quicksand.

- Instead, slowly wriggle your legs a little, advises Bonn. This creates space for water to flow, which will loosen up the sand.

- Another way to escape from quicksand, especially if you are in up to your waist, is to slowly lean back. That will take some weight off your feet and loosen the sand's grip. Once you are floating on your back, carefully roll over onto your stomach. Use your hands to pull yourself across the quicksand to solid ground.

- Whatever you do, take your time. If you move too quickly, you could agitate the soil, which might create new pockets of quicksand.

CREEPY CREATURES

RATS

FRIGHT METER

Rats give most people a serious case of the heebie-jeebies. One glimpse of a beady-eyed, yellow-toothed rodent the size of a small cat scuttling across your basement floor—or one night spent listening to a family of them thrashing around inside the walls of your house—is enough to make most people run, screaming.

What makes rats so scary? The answer probably goes back to the 1300s when a deadly infection known as the bubonic plague killed a third of the population of Europe. Fleas that lived on rats spread the disease. While the bubonic plague is unlikely to happen again, rats do still carry bacteria and viruses that cause illness

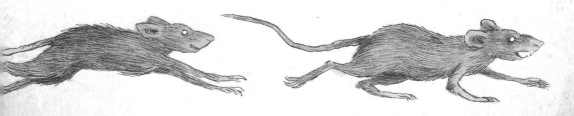

The bubonic plague—not a good time to be a European.

(although pigeons do a much better job of it), so for that reason alone, it's a good idea to keep your distance from them.

But something else makes people's hair stand on end when they see a rat. It could be all the stories they've heard: "Rats like to bite people." "They can swim up into your toilet." "Someday they will take over the Earth."

When it comes to the brown rat (sometimes called the Norway rat or sewer rat), some of the scariest stories are actually true. There are more than 400 different kinds of rats in the world. Most like to keep their distance from humans, but not brown rats. These guys like to live close to people—they especially love cities, where there is a nonstop buffet of garbage to dine on.

In most cities, you won't ever see rats, but they are right there, under your feet. They live in huge colonies under sidewalks, in sewer systems, and in subway tunnels. A few unlucky commuters in New York City have even witnessed a rat board a train,

A VERY, *VERY* LARGE RAT

The average brown rat is about 16 inches long and weighs one pound. If conditions are good, they can grow to be 20 inches long and weigh two pounds. But that's tiny compared to the Mallomys giant rat, which was discovered in 2009 by a TV film crew at an extinct volcano in Papua New Guinea.

The 32-inch-long rat weighed 3.3 pounds and showed no fear of humans. It's thought to be one of the biggest in the world, and it's a "true rat, the same kind you find in city sewers," according to scientists. Don't worry about meeting it on the street, though: The Mallomys rat lives only in the area of the volcano.

race around the car, and then get off at the next stop, leaving its fellow passengers shrieking.

But we digress. What about the toilets? And the biting? And the taking over the Earth? Here are the cold, beady-eyed facts about rats.

1. **They *can* swim up into toilet bowls.** Rats are very good swimmers—in fact, they can swim for three days without stopping. Which means they can paddle through the sewers and pop up in someone's toilet—or bathtub, as one New York City resident discovered when he came home from work one day to a large, frantic rat racing around inside his tub.

2. **Rats *do* bite people . . . occasionally.** When a rat is cornered, it will bite—and it will bite *hard*. A rat's front teeth are very long (they can grow five inches every year) and very sharp. They are stronger than iron, and when a rat bites down, its jaw exerts as much as 7,000 pounds of pressure. A scientist who had a rat bite his finger reported that the animal's teeth went right through the bone. Ouch!

Occasionally, where there are heavy infestations, rats will bite people's faces and hands at night while they sleep, drawn by food residue on their skin. That might be a good time to move to a new place. Once a rat bites you, your chances of being bitten again go way up. It's like going back to a favorite restaurant, from the rat's point of view. A scientist who fed lab rats human blood in the 1940s concluded that rats can develop "a real craving for fresh human blood."

3. **It's *really* hard to get rid of rats.** They may not take over the Earth someday, but rats do have an incredible ability to survive and multiply. They can squeeze through

WHAT'S SO FUNNY?
Rats are noisy. They squeak, shriek, and hiss. They also make high-pitched chirping sounds that humans cannot hear, but which scientists think may be the equivalent of laughter.

holes the size of a quarter by collapsing their skeletons, lift objects that weigh more than a pound, or chew right through a wall—even if it's made of brick, cement, or lead.

You can try to get rid of rats with poison, but they are very smart. They will eat just a tiny bit of a new food to make sure it doesn't make them sick. Then there is the new strain of rat that scientists call "genetically mutated super rats." These guys are immune to almost every kind of poison. The only sure way to get rid of rats in a home is to throw away the food and garbage they feed on.

In the big picture, rats are here to stay. They multiply so fast that even if some die, there will be plenty of others—thousands—to take their place. One female rat can have as many as 240 babies a year, and since some of those rats will have babies, too, it's possible for a pair of rats to produce 15,000 descendants in one year.

4. **Where there is one rat, there are *many*.** Rats are very sociable and they nest in large groups. If they are disturbed, they will run in a huge mass. If you happen to be in their

path, climb up a wall. When threatened they will turn on a predator together.

5. **Rats have a super smart leader called the "rat king."** *False! Whew.* But don't get too relaxed. There is something called a "rat king," only it's not one rat—it's a mess of rats whose tails have become knotted together in their nest. A rat king can contain as many as 32 rats. Since they can't go out looking for food, sometimes other rats feed the rat king until it eventually dies.

SANDBOX TREE

FRIGHT METER

The sandbox tree's trunk is covered with sharp spikes that practically scream "Step away from the tree. Step away *now*!" The painful pokers, which give the tree the nickname "monkey-no-climb," are just the beginning. This tree's leaves, bark, and sap are all poisonous. The sap in particular is so toxic that it is used in Mexico to make poison arrows that can kill fish.

If you find yourself in parts of Asia or Central or South America where this tree grows, you should keep your distance. But even that may not keep you safe. The sandbox has an explosive secret weapon that gives it its other nickname: "dynamite tree." When the tree's pumpkin-shaped fruits are ripe, they burst open with a loud bang and shoot poisonous seeds as far as 300 feet— about the length of a football field. The poison in the seed is not enough to kill you, but the seeds launch at 150 miles per hour and

can hit with enough force to
injure a person.

Even if the bulletlike pods don't hit you, they
can terrify you. A man living in Cambodia was awakened in the
middle of the night by what sounded like a gun being fired into
his bedroom. He heard the sound of breaking glass and pieces
of wood clattering to the floor. He leaped up in terror, thinking
someone was invading his home, only to find the culprit was
seedpods shot from a nearby sandbox tree.

SIX OF THE DEADLIEST PLANTS IN THE WORLD

These plants don't look scary, but they all have the capacity to kill. Don't put any of them in a bouquet—or in your mouth!

CASTOR OIL PLANT

Many people plant this shrub in their garden. Its purple and green leaves are lovely, but its seeds, which look like beans, contain ricin, one of the most lethal substances in the world. Ricin kills by interfering with the function of individual cells in your body. Eventually your organs fail—and so do you.

DEADLY NIGHTSHADE

This bushy plant produces shiny black berries the size of cherries that beg to be tasted. The fruit is delightfully sweet—and not-so-delightfully deadly. The berries (along with other parts of the plant) contain two chemicals that cause paralysis in some muscles—including the heart muscle, where the effect is fatal.

WATER HEMLOCK

This lacy wildflower is a cousin of hemlock, the plant that famously killed the Greek philosopher Socrates. Called "the most violently toxic plant in North America," water hemlock contains cicutoxin, a chemical

that causes painful convulsions, nausea, and often death if you make the mistake of eating it.

ACONITE

Also called monkshood, wolfsbane, or devil's helmet, this purple-flowered plant grows in the foothills of Europe and Asia. Every inch of the plant contains

aconitine, a poison that makes your mouth burn and then causes drooling, vomiting, and ultimately, death. The ancient Greeks put aconite on the tips of arrows used to kill wolves. In *Harry Potter and the Prisoner of Azkaban*, Professor Snape uses aconite brew to help keep Professor Lupin from turning into a werewolf.

WHITE SNAKEROOT

This North American herb with tiny white flowers is blamed for killing Abraham Lincoln's mother. She didn't eat the plant—she drank milk from a cow that ate it. Fortunately, farmers now make sure there is not a sprig of this lethal herb in their pastures.

ROSARY PEA

Found in tropical areas, including Florida, the rosary pea produces beautiful red and black seeds that contain abrin, perhaps one of the most lethal plant poisons in the world. The amount of abrin contained in a single seed is enough to kill a human. The seeds are dangerous only if broken or scratched, but some jewelry makers who create necklaces from the seeds have died after accidentally pricking their fingers while on the job.

SÉANCE

FRIGHT METER

Six well-dressed men and women are seated around a table in the darkened parlor of an old house. The curtains are drawn and the only light comes from flickering candles on the table. The friends watch as one man appears to enter a trance. All of a sudden his mouth opens and he begins to speak. His voice is high and sweet—the voice of a woman. It's as if a stranger is speaking through him.

"I miss you all very much," the voice says. "Tell me, is my husband okay? And my children?"

Suddenly the table tilts to one side, seemingly by itself. Everyone gasps. Was it the spirit of the woman whose voice they heard, moving through the room?

This eerie meeting, called a séance, took place more than 100 years ago. A séance is a gathering of people who wish to communicate with the dead, sometimes with the help of a medium, a person who claims to be able to receive messages from ghosts or spirits. Some say the spirits communicate by using the medium's vocal cords to "speak."

BIRTH OF A FRIGHTENING FAD

Séances have been around since ancient times, but they became hugely popular in the mid-1800s, thanks to two girls from Hydesville, New York. On a March night in 1848, 14-year-old Margaret Fox and her 11-year-old sister, Kate, tried talking to a ghost they believed lived in their family's house.

Kate and Margaret Fox with their older sister, Leah, left.

The ghost reportedly responded with knocking sounds: one knock for "yes" and two knocks for "no." After asking a series of questions, the girls concluded they were "speaking" to the ghost of a man named Charles Rosa, who had been murdered.

Word spread that the Fox sisters were mediums who could communicate with the dead, and they became instant celebrities. They traveled all over the United States performing séances in front of packed audiences. During their shows, spirits would not only tap out messages but objects would move by themselves—proof, said the Foxes, that ghosts were on stage.

The Fox sisters sparked a movement called "spiritualism," the belief that the dead can communicate with the living. Thousands of people in the United States and Europe began holding séances at home, and business boomed for the Foxes and other mediums who made money doing séances on stage. Many performed physical feats to demonstrate that the spirits were present—they made bells ring, levitated objects, or got the spirits to "write" messages on a piece of slate.

A medium named Daniel Dunglas Home reportedly levitated his own body during séances throughout the 1860s. At one session, witnesses claimed he rose several feet off the ground, exited through a large window, and floated back in through another window.

Another medium named Marthe Béraud would conduct séances where she went into a trance and ejected gobs of white stuff from her mouth. She called the material "ectoplasm" and said it was a spiritual substance that proved that a dead person was communicating through her. Scientists said it proved something else: Béraud was a fraud. When they examined the "ectoplasm," they discovered it was simply white fabric.

"Ectoplasm" pouring out of medium Marthe Béraud's mouth.

BELIEVERS VS. SKEPTICS

Many people believed that séances worked, though skeptics argued that they were just theatrical tricks played on people who were very willing to be fooled. Professional magicians, including the famous escape artist Harry Houdini, exposed mediums who borrowed the tools and techniques of magic to hoodwink their audiences.

Scientists also tried to convince the public that séances were nonsense. In 1852, physicist Michael Faraday did an experiment that explained how a table could appear to tip by itself. He discovered the ideomotor effect: A person's thoughts can make their muscles move involuntarily, without their knowledge. When a group of people at a séance place their hands on a table and are expecting that the table might move by itself, it will move because their muscles will involuntarily respond to the idea.

DO SÉANCES WORK?

In 1888, 40 years after the Fox sisters started the craze for séances, they admitted that they had faked their spirits' knocking sounds by cracking the joints of their big toes. The public's enthusiasm for séances continued through the early 1900s and then finally died down.

But séances never disappeared entirely. Today, people still conduct them in hopes of contacting the dead, usually by channeling spoken messages.

The debate about whether or not séances work lives on, too.

Can the living really communicate with the dead? Or does it just seem that way when you are in a darkened room and everything you see or hear seems eerie and otherworldly?

Decide for yourself. Try conducting your own séance using the tips on page 142 and see if any unexpected guests show up.

HOLD YOUR OWN
SÉANCE

FRIGHT METER

Important! Get permission from a parent before having a séance. And never invite very young children or anyone who is easily frightened.

HORRIFYING HOW-TO

WHAT YOU NEED

- Two or more people (in addition to yourself) who believe it *may* be possible to communicate with spirits.

- A room that is quiet—without any TV, music, or other distractions

- A table, preferably round or oval

- A chair for each participant
- A small lamp (or candles, if a parent is present)
- A glass of water
- A pad of paper and a pencil

WHAT YOU DO

1. Prepare the room

Place the table in the center of the room and arrange the chairs around it.

Place the small lamp (or candle if your parent says it's okay and agrees to light it) in the center of the table along with the glass of water and the paper and pencil.

Turn out any overhead lights and close the curtains or shades if it is daytime.

2. "Cleanse" the room

Some people say it's a good idea to create a pleasant scent in the room to get rid of "negative energy" that could discourage spirits from entering. When your guests arrive, ask them to help you "cleanse" the room by walking in a circle carrying something with a strong but nice odor. You can use a bowl containing crushed orange peel and a few drops of vanilla extract or a stick of incense if your parent says it's okay.

3. Choose a medium and a spirit

Invite your guests to be seated at the table and pick a "medium." This is the person who will receive messages from beyond. You can offer to go first and then let others take turns being the medium.

Think of a famous person who is no longer living and whose spirit you want to contact. Discuss what questions you want to ask the person. It's best to ask yes or no questions. Explain to everyone that if the water in the glass moves, it could be a sign that a spirit is asking you to listen.

-CONTINUED-

4. Begin the séance

Have everyone close their eyes and take slow, deep breaths to relax. When you feel calm, ask everyone to place their hands on the table and join hands.

Chant together: "Dear [name of spirit], beloved spirit, please move among us and speak through us. We welcome you with open minds and hearts." Stay very still and listen for any sounds that might signal a spirit is trying to reach you. Also watch the glass of water for any movements, another possible sign of communication.

If you see or hear signs that the spirit may be listening, the medium should ask a question and wait for another response. If you are the medium, close your eyes and relax as much as possible so you will notice any words or phrases flitting across your mind that might be messages. Repeat whatever you hear to the group—or write it on the pad of paper—even if it doesn't make sense. It might just be a single word.

You can also direct the spirit to respond by making a tapping noise: once for "yes," twice for "no."

Continue to ask questions as long as you get responses. You may not receive any responses at all. Some people say that's because the spirit is not ready to communicate and you should try again later. Skeptics say it's because séances don't work. You will have to decide for yourself. Whether or not your séance works, it can be thrillingly creepy just to try summoning spirits from beyond.

5. End the séance

When you are ready to stop, thank the spirits by chanting together three times:

"Thank you, dear spirit, now leave in peace."

SHARKS

FRIGHT METER

*J*aws. This word is likely one of the first things that comes to mind when you think of sharks—especially the most famous of the over 400 shark species, the great white shark.

These ocean hunters are built for detecting and devouring prey. In addition to having incredibly sharp eyesight and hearing, they have electroreceptors on their noses that let them sense the vibrations of nearby animals that might make a good snack. Speaking

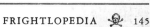

of sharp senses, some sharks can detect tiny amounts of blood from hundreds of feet away—about the length of several football fields.

They waste no time getting to the snack once they sense it. Sharks are covered with small scales called dermal denticles that help them move quickly through the water. Similar to tiny teeth, these scales are very sharp and offer protection as well. Most sharks swim at speeds of about five miles per hour, but some are faster. The shortfin mako shark zips along at more than 20 miles per hour and has been clocked at more than 40 miles per hour.

Then there are those teeth. Up to 300 sharp, jagged, triangular teeth fill a great white shark's mouth, arranged in several rows. Over time, the teeth fall out one by one and are replaced with new, equally sharp chompers. Sharks may go through up to 20,000 teeth in a lifetime. On the rare occasions when these ocean hunters come into contact with human swimmers, they will usually inspect the person and then move on. But it might be a toothy, painful, and rather bloody inspection.

Think you're in the clear as long as you're far away from the ocean? Think again. While most sharks are ocean dwellers, bull sharks have a high tolerance for low salt levels and have been found in rivers around the world, including the Mississippi.

REASONS TO LOVE SHARKS

Sharks have a bad rap when it comes to people. If anything, sharks have more to fear from humans than vice versa. Many species are endangered or at risk of becoming endangered soon, mainly because people hunt them for their meat and fins, which are considered a delicacy.

SNAKES

FRIGHT METER

Just say the word *snake* while walking through the woods with friends and you can probably get at least one person to scream "*Where?!*" and start running.

Snakes slither. Snakes have fangs. And snakes can kill you (well, some of them can). Those three things make these ancient reptiles scary to a lot of people—in fact more people suffer from ophidiophobia (fear of snakes) than almost any other phobia in the world.

The truth is, most of the 3,000 species of snakes in the world are harmless to humans. *Most.* A few are *not* harmless. They are the ones that give all snakes a bad rap. Here are several you should definitely be afraid of.

SIX SNAKES YOU DO NOT WANT TO MESS WITH

BLACK MAMBA

WHERE IT LIVES: Southern and Eastern Africa

WHAT IT LOOKS LIKE: The black mamba is actually brown, not black. Its name comes from the color of the inside of its mouth, which it shows when threatened. It's the longest venomous snake in Africa, and can reach 14 feet long.

WHY YOU SHOULD BE AFRAID: This snake is very aggressive about defending its territory.

When it feels threatened, it lifts its head and as much as a third of its body off the ground, opens its black mouth, and hisses. If whatever is bothering it doesn't skedaddle, the snake strikes not just once, but many times in a row, injecting some of the most powerful venom in the world. The venom packs a double wallop: It causes paralysis and it stops the heart. Just two drops are enough to kill a human.

ONE MORE SCARY FACT: The black mamba is the fastest snake in the world. It can zip along at

In 2010, a man spent four months in a locked room with 40 venomous snakes at a reptile park in South Africa. He set a record—and he didn't get bitten once.

up to 12 miles per hour, faster than most humans can run. Seeing one race by with its head nearly four feet up in the air is a horrifying sight for some people. Luckily, black mambas use their speed to get away from danger, not to chase down prey.

REASONS TO LOVE SNAKES

A few snakes are worth steering clear of, but most snakes are harmless to humans and won't attack unless provoked. Often, snakes do a lot of good. When an area has many snakes, it's a sign that the environment is healthy. Rattlesnakes help people by eating pests like rats and mice. Some snakes' venom contains compounds that can lower blood pressure and may have the potential to cure certain cancers.

RATTLESNAKE

WHERE IT LIVES: Throughout the Americas, from Canada to Argentina

WHAT IT LOOKS LIKE: The rattlesnake has a heavy body, a diamond-shaped head, and—as its name says—a rattle on its tail.

WHY YOU SHOULD BE AFRAID: A rattlesnake bite is unlikely to kill you, but it can cause a terrible, burning pain that one biologist said is like being branded. The snake's hollow fangs deliver a type of venom that digests flesh and causes bleeding inside the body—which is why the pain is so severe.

ONE MORE SCARY FACT: You should always steer clear of a rattlesnake that has recently been killed. Up to an hour after a rattlesnake head has been severed from the body, it can still flick its tongue and bite.

INLAND TAIPAN

WHERE IT LIVES: Australia

WHAT IT LOOKS LIKE: Dark brown in the winter, straw-colored in the summer, the inland taipan is usually about five feet long but can grow up to eight feet.

WHY YOU SHOULD BE AFRAID: Drop for drop, this snake's venom is the most deadly in the world. It is estimated that the venom in one bite could kill 100 people (luckily, it prefers rats). The inland taipan is extremely fast and accurate, and can strike more than once in a single attack.

ONE MORE SCARY FACT: The inland taipan's venom contains a "spreading factor" that makes a victim's body absorb the poison faster.

AFRICAN ROCK PYTHON

WHERE IT LIVES: Africa

WHAT IT LOOKS LIKE: The largest snake in Africa, the rock

WHY YOU SHOULD BE AFRAID:
The African rock python is very aggressive and lightning-fast. It grabs its prey with its long, curved teeth, wraps its massive body around the creature, and squeezes with enormous force. Each time the prey breathes out, the snake tightens its coils until it strangulates the animal. Then the python swallows the victim

python can weigh a whopping 200 pounds. The snake's body is yellowish, gray-brown, or gray-green with a whitish belly.

THE WORLD'S LARGEST GATHERING OF SNAKES

If you are trying to confront your fear of snakes, a visit to Manitoba, Canada, during the spring may do the trick—or it might send you right over the edge. Every year during mating season, about 75,000 garter snakes gather in the Narcissee Snake Dens, a series of limestone caves. The snakes form squirming masses called "mating balls," made up of about 100 male snakes that are trying to win the affections of a single female. The snakes are harmless, but if you startle them, they have an unpleasant way of getting you to leave: They emit a fluid that isn't poop, but smells just as bad.

whole—even if it's an antelope, which is much bigger than the snake's head.

ONE MORE SCARY FACT: Rock pythons are so fast and so powerful that they can kill a crocodile.

SPITTING COBRA

WHERE IT LIVES: Africa and Asia

WHAT IT LOOKS LIKE: There are several species of spitting cobras. They range from four feet long to more than nine feet and their skin can be gray, yellow, pink, or brown. All have the distinctive hood of a cobra.

WHY YOU SHOULD BE AFRAID: When threatened, the spitting cobra ejects venom from a hole in its fangs and can hit a target up to eight feet away. The snake often aims for the face, a smart move because the venom is harmless when it lands on your skin, but causes a horrible, burning pain when it gets in your eyes. If not treated, it can cause blindness.

ONE MORE SCARY FACT: Spitting cobras can also deliver venom through a bite. The largest species, Ashe's spitting cobra, is thought to deliver more venom with a single bite than any other cobra in the world.

FLYING SNAKE

WHERE IT LIVES: Southeast Asia

WHAT IT LOOKS LIKE: There are five species of flying snake. The biggest can grow up to four feet long. They come in many colors, from black with green, red, and orange, to pure yellow or green.

WHY YOU SHOULD BE AFRAID: Most snakes slither along the ground. If you step carefully, you can avoid them. But the flying

snake can climb up a tree and then fling itself off and glide through the air, twisting and turning to ride the air currents. The snake can land on another tree, the ground, or perhaps, if you are extremely unlucky, your head.

ONE MORE SCARY FACT: One species of flying snake, the paradise tree snake, can travel 300 feet (the length of a soccer field) in the air.

STINGING TREE

FRIGHT METER

"**W**ouldn't you like to taste a sweet, juicy raspberry?" The stinging tree (which can measure anywhere from three to 15 feet tall) beckons with clusters of bright red fruit that look a lot like raspberries. Don't take the bait.

The stinging tree is called the most feared plant in Australia for a reason. If you so much as brush against the leaves, tiny silicon hairs that contain a powerful toxin enter your skin and cause a pain so severe that some people actually have a heart attack when they first get "stung." There is not much you can do except scream in agony, because

the fine hairs are almost impossible to remove. The pain can last for as long as a year, and touching your skin can reactivate the toxin.

A brush with danger: The tiny hairs on the stinging tree pack a painful punch.

Wearing protective clothing doesn't even help, because the tiny hairs of the stinging tree can pass right through fabric. In 1941, a soldier reportedly fell into a stinging tree and his whole body got covered with the plant's hairs. The poor guy had to be tied to his hospital bed for three weeks because the pain was so horrible.

Of course no plant has evil intentions, but it's hard to believe the stinging tree isn't out to get people when you consider this additional fact: The tree constantly releases its toxic hairs into the air, where passersby can breathe them in or get them in their eyes. It's enough to make you walk around in a hazmat suit if you're visiting the rain forests of Eastern Australia.

STONEFISH

FRIGHT METER

If you ever visit the beautiful beaches of Australia, you might want to bring some steel-soled boots. Australia is home to the stonefish, a bug-eyed, warty sea creature that delivers the most painful sting in the animal world.

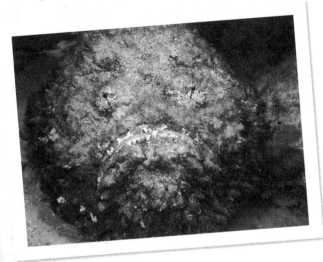

The stonefish has 13 spiny fins on its back, and when you step on one of them, it feels like a burning hot needle has been plunged into your foot. What's actually entering your body is a dose of extremely toxic venom. As the poison

EAT IT IF YOU DARE!

Stonefish are not fun to step on, but they can make a delicious meal. In Japan, the venomous fish is served both cooked and raw. It's safe for diners because the venomous fins are removed before it's served. But chefs must be careful—at least one cook ended up in the emergency room after getting venom in a cut in his finger while cutting a stonefish.

seeps in, your foot swells up like a balloon and the pain shoots up your leg—and quickly becomes unbearable. According to people who have been stung, it feels like someone is pounding your leg for hours with a sledgehammer.

The stonefish sounds like a good fish to avoid, right? Good luck! This creature is a master of deception. Its crusty skin blends in perfectly with the ocean's coral and stones (hence its name). When the fish comes up on the beach, it uses its fins to bury itself partway in the sand so you can barely see it. The stonefish can survive out of the water for several hours, invisible to beachgoers.

In order to teach their children about the dangers of stonefish, aboriginal people of Australia invented a dance. First, they put a clay model of the stonefish in the water. Then a dancer dives in, steps on the clay fish, and starts screaming in agony. Finally, the performer writhes on the ground and "dies" to the sound of a death song.

If you are unlucky enough to step on a stonefish, you probably won't do it a second time because you will never forget the pain. Luckily, doctors can give you a shot of antivenom that will keep the poison from killing you—if the pain doesn't.

TASMANIAN DEVIL

FRIGHT METER

If you ever find yourself face to face with an angry Tasmanian devil, one look at the huge, razor-sharp teeth inside its mouth will make you want to run. And run you should. These fierce little guys have teeth so sharp they can break through bones and thick hides. Mostly they keep to themselves—and the smaller creatures they hunt—but if they feel threatened they will attack a human.

About the size of a beagle, Tasmanian devils live on the Australian island state of Tasmania. They eat insects, snakes, birds, and

Tasmanian devils were once found all over Australia, but now live only in Tasmania, where they build their dens in dry, wooded areas.

other small animals. And when we say they eat these animals, we mean they Eat. These. Animals. T-devils leave very little behind at the end of a meal, devouring their prey's hair, bones, organs, and everything in between. And they are not quiet diners. While they feast, they let out loud, high-pitched screams and snorting sounds. The volume of a Tasmanian devil's noises lets everyone know who is boss at mealtime.

If you're on the Tasmanian devil's most-wanted list of possible meals, watch out. Rather than chase its prey through the woods, the T-devil might fake a yawn as its next victim is passing by. Then, *Bam!* It snaps up its small, meaty snack with its super-sharp teeth. Tasmanian devils can be dangerous, but they are not known to attack humans unless they feel threatened. If you are upright, you are probably safe. However, if you're looking for a place to nap, try not to lie out in the middle of the Tasmanian bush. Then you might be in trouble.

REASONS TO LOVE TASMANIAN DEVILS

Scary as they look, Tasmanian devils are actually rather timid around humans, and these days, they need our protection. In the 1800s, farmers believed (incorrectly) that Tasmanian devils were killing off their livestock, so they started hunting them and nearly wiped them out. Around 1940, the population was back up, but then in the 1990s the species fell victim to a fatal cancer called devil facial tumor disease (DFTD). Ever since then, wildlife groups have worked hard to find a cure and save this endangered animal.

TRANSYLVANIA

Transylvania. The word alone sounds creepy. It conjures up visions of a land of dark, forbidding forests, ghost-ridden castle ruins, and, of course, Dracula. Transylvania is indeed the fictional home of the world's most famous vampire. It's also a real place, a region in the Eastern European country of Romania, full of medieval towns and gorgeous landscapes—and some sites that may give you the chills.

TARGOVISTE CASTLE

A prince named Vlad Tepes ruled Transylvania during the 1400s, and was either a great leader or a brutal murderer, depending on whom you ask. Vlad lived in Targoviste Castle during his reign, and he made a real name for himself: Vlad the Impaler. He killed many thousands of people—basically anyone who opposed him—by having them impaled (yes, with stakes). Some people believe that the ghosts of Vlad's tens of thousands of victims have stuck around to haunt the castle.

HUNYAD CASTLE

When Vlad's reign ended in 1462, he was thrown in an underground prison in Hunyad Castle, and some say his phantom still resides in the enormous fortress. In 2013, the hosts of a TV show about ghosts went to the castle to investigate. A tour guide brought them to the cell where Vlad had been held hundreds of years ago. They called out, looking for signs of a supernatural presence. Although no one answered, they claimed they felt a rush of cold air, which also registered on their detection equipment. Was it the ghost of Vlad Tepes? Or just the natural coolness of a stone dungeon?

HOIA BACIU FOREST

Many people consider Transylvania's Hoia Baciu Forest to be the scariest forest on Earth. Residents warn visitors that if they enter the woods there is no guarantee they will come out. Over the years, people have reported hearing voices and spotting UFOs, unexplained lights, and strange-looking trees with curved trunks. But the most dangerous area of all is "the circle," a clearing inside the forest where no trees grow. Some say this area is a hangout for ghosts or other paranormal forces. Would you dare visit to find out?

UFOS AND ALIENS

If you ever spot a weird light or shape in the sky and just can't figure out what it is, you may start to wonder: Could it be a spaceship from another planet—or even another galaxy? Who, or what, is on board? Do they come in peace?

In the mid-1900s, reports of Unidentified Flying Objects (UFOs) suddenly took off. Many of the sightings were later explained by the weather or other not-so-exciting happenings, but some remain a mystery. It's those still unexplained objects that keep believers watching the skies.

FAMOUS UFO SIGHTINGS

Here are three of the best-known UFO "sightings" in history. No one can prove they are real, but they do make out-of-this-world stories.

WHEN: July 1947

WHERE: Roswell, New Mexico

WHAT: UFO landing

WHAT HAPPENED: Several people claimed they saw a huge flying disc that had crashed just outside of Roswell, New Mexico. A rancher in the area reported finding several metal sticks taped together in his sheep pasture. He called the local sheriff, who alerted the Roswell Army Air Field (RAAF).

The local newspaper reported "RAAF Captures Flying Saucer on Ranch in Roswell Region,"

but hours later, the military said that inspection of the wreckage showed it was nothing more than a weather balloon. Yet, curiously, the military added that the wreckage was being sent to an airfield for "further inspection."

Many continued to believe the object was a UFO, especially when witnesses claimed the pieces of recovered metal did not behave like "regular" metal or foil.

Mac Brazel, a rancher who lived in the area, said when he folded or crumpled some of the material, it returned to its original shape.

Around the same time, just a couple of miles away, another crash was reported, along with sightings of nonhuman crash victims. They were described as creatures four to five feet tall with large heads, oversized eyes, and small mouths. Many people believed they were aliens. Some said later that they were told by government officials not to talk about what they had seen.

THE EXPLANATION: Decades later, in the 1990s, the government offered more information about the crash wreckage found near Roswell. It said that the metal debris did come from a weather balloon, but it wasn't being used to study the weather: It was used to monitor the Soviet Union (now Russia) to see if their military was conducting bomb tests.

As for the "alien" bodies seen near Roswell, until long after the crash, the government said they were dummies used in parachute experiments.

This explanation satisfied some people, but many still believe a UFO crashed in Roswell that summer, and they will probably never be convinced that the events of July 1947 were anything other than an attempted alien invasion.

WHEN: July 1952

WHERE: Washington, D.C.

WHAT: Mysterious lights

WHAT HAPPENED: Air traffic controllers at Washington National Airport were surprised to see seven unexpected blips on their radar screens that were unlike the movements that aircraft normally make. The workers' surprise turned to alarm when they learned that operators at two nearby air force bases had made similar observations.

Meanwhile, a pilot who was flying nearby reported seeing lights that looked "like falling stars without tails" and many people reported similar sightings from the ground. According to some, the UFOs hovered above the nation's Capitol building for several hours and radar detected them moving at almost 900 miles per hour.

THE EXPLANATION: During July 1952, Washington, D.C., was experiencing hotter-than-usual weather. Some experts said the extreme heat caused the blips. Others maintained that the sightings were truly unidentified or, as they put it, "unknowns." An exact cause for this event has still not been found, and we may never know for sure. What do *you* think it was?

WHEN: September 1961

WHERE: New Hampshire

WHAT: Alien abduction

WHAT HAPPENED: Driving home to New Hampshire from a trip to Canada, Barney and Betty Hill saw something unusual flying through the night sky. Barney looked through his binoculars and thought he saw a long, narrow spacecraft moving alongside the road and being operated by some kind of creature. The Hills also heard some strange beeping sounds, and according to some reports, pulled over to investigate when they saw a mysterious light. To add to the weirdness, the Hills' trip home took hours longer than it should have, but the next day, neither of them could account for the extra time that had passed.

Barney and Betty tried to go about their lives, but they had nightmares and frightening memories of their creepy trip. They reported noticing more bizarre happenings. Betty saw a powdery substance on the dress she had been wearing during their trip home. Strange circles appeared on their car the day after their drive back. Barney's shoes were inexplicably scratched up, and their watches stopped working—permanently.

Eventually the Hills concluded that during their drive, aliens had abducted them from their car, brought them aboard a UFO, and examined them—which explained why their trip took longer than it should have.

If that's not enough to scare you, consider this: When Betty reported the incident, officials at the local air force base said that they, too, had seen "something" that same night.

THE EXPLANATION: No one has been able to prove or disprove that aliens abducted the Hills. But some researchers question the Hills' explanation. They found contradictions between Betty and Barney's versions of the story, and over time, their account of what happened that September night changed.

UFO ALIEN MESSAGE

FRIGHT METER

A UFO just landed near your house and the aliens inside said something in their weird language. Use the key to decode the message.

HORRIFYING HOW-TO

KEY:

A = E	H = L	O = S	V = Z
B = F	I = M	P = T	W = A
C = G	J = N	Q = U	X = B
D = H	K = O	R = V	Y = C
E = I	L = P	S = W	Z = D
F = J	M = Q	T = X	
G = K	N = R	U = Y	

ALIEN MESSAGE: SA DWRA YKIA PK CAP UKQ!

__ _____ _____ __

___ ____!

URBAN LEGENDS

FRIGHT METER

Have you ever heard the story about the alligator that crawled up out of the toilet into someone's house? It's an urban legend—a horrific and often barely plausible story that gets passed from one person to another until people start to think it's true.

Here are some creepy urban legends you can use to scare your friends. Add your own details to make the stories fit the place where you live. Or, invent your own.

- My cousin's neighbor was attacked by her pet cat in the middle of the night. When she woke up the next morning, she had a light coat of fur growing all over her body.

- A man who lives on our street bought a used car. After he got it, he found out that someone was once murdered in it. Now, in the middle of the night, the car backs out of the driveway and drives around the block. When you look in the driver's seat, no one's there.

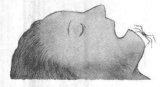

- My mother had a spider crawl into her mouth in the middle of the night and she swallowed it. They pumped her stomach a week later and it was full of spider eggs.

- My friend's grandfather accidentally buried his dog before it was really dead. For years after, you could hear the dog howling in the middle of the night. It wouldn't stop until the man left a bowl of food near its grave. He finally had to move away. He was losing his mind.

- If you pee in certain lakes or rivers, a tiny parasitic fish can swim up inside you and eat you from the inside out.

- A kid hid his Halloween candy in the back of the closet and didn't eat any of it for weeks because he wanted it to last for a long time. When he finally went to get some, he was horrified to see the bag moving around by itself and giving off a weird green light. It turned out that a pregnant rat had been living inside the bag. It ate so much rotting candy that it gave birth to mutant babies. They had multiple heads and gave off a sickly greenish glow.

CREEPY CREATURES

VAMPIRE BATS

FRIGHT METER

Most bats are not nearly as scary as many people believe. But vampire bats are a different matter. For starters, the word *vampire* is in their name for a reason. Most bats eat fruit and nectar, but these guys prefer a meal of warm blood. They use their sharp teeth to pierce the thick skin of cows, horses, other livestock, and sometimes birds. Then they slurp up the blood. Venom in their saliva keeps the blood from clotting so it doesn't get too thick and gooey as they drink.

REASONS TO LOVE VAMPIRE BATS

Like other bats, vampire bats don't prey on humans. Scientists even believe that vampire bat venom could be helpful in treating people who have had strokes, because it helps prevent blood clots.

GIDDYUP, LIL' BAT

Like all bats, vampire bats send out sound waves to locate their prey and fly over for a meal. Unlike most bats, vampire bats can also walk—and even gallop. As they fly, heat sensors on their noses help them identify the right time to strike, then they land on the ground and approach their prey on foot.

A vampire bat's bite doesn't cause immediate pain, but it can lead to infections and disease—so this is a bat you should definitely avoid. That shouldn't be too hard: Only three out of more than 1,200 bat species are vampire bats. They live mostly in Mexico, Central America, and South America.

VAMPIRE BITE

W ant to look like you just got a fresh vampire bite? Follow these instructions from makeup artist Ramy and make your friends and family think that you were a vampire's latest victim. Ouch! Use this trick at Halloween or anytime you want to horrify your household.

HORRIFYING HOW-TO

WHAT YOU NEED

- A red lip pencil
- A black eyeliner pencil
- Translucent face powder (optional)
- An adult to help

Note: You can buy these materials at a local beauty or party supply store, or have an adult order them online.

1. Using the red lip pencil, draw two dots on your neck, roughly an inch or two apart. Then use the pencil to make the dots a little bigger than the pencil's point.

2. Using the black eyeliner pencil, outline the dots, going only halfway around each dot.

3. (Optional) If you have translucent powder, pat some over the bite marks.

4. Using the red lip pencil, you can make the bite wounds "bleed" by drawing wiggly lines down your neck, starting at the red dots.

VAMPIRES

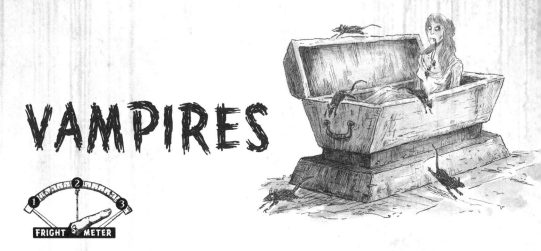

FRIGHT METER

Sometimes referred to as the "undead," vampires are mythical creatures that leave their graves at night to feed off the living. What makes them even scarier is that they are not always easy to spot. In many stories and movies, vampires live among normal, everyday people. They talk, eat, and even socialize as if they are "one of us." At first glance, they seem like regular folks, but regular they are *not.* Most notably, their favorite beverage is human blood, and they get it by sinking their sharp fangs into human necks.

Legends vary and vampire folklore is always changing, but vampires usually have some other peculiar features that set them apart: They can't see their own reflection in a mirror. They have a habit of sleeping in coffins during daylight. They are often incredibly strong, extremely fast, and have sharp senses, especially when it comes to smelling and hearing. Many vampires can read minds, which comes in handy when they're stalking a victim. And while vampires are not alive, they can hang around for several centuries.

THE TRANSFORMATION

By most accounts, becoming a vampire is a pretty straightforward process. Basically all you have to do is get bitten by a vampire who drinks some of your blood, then you take a bite of that vampire, and boom, you're in. Some say you can also enter vampire-dom by being buried with your mouth open or having a cat jump over your dead body just before you're lowered into the grave.

EXTRA GARLIC, PLEASE

If you're not keen on becoming a vampire (or victim), there are several ways to stave off—or kill—these creepy creatures of the night. Here are some of the most effective methods.

RELIGIOUS SYMBOLS

In general, religion and vampires don't mix. For example, in Bram Stoker's novel *Dracula,* a crucifix and holy water, which are sacred to some Christian religions, are used to keep vampires at bay.

GARLIC

The onion's little cousin is also a popular vampire antidote. It's a

> *In Poland, people used to bury loved ones with a sickle (a large, curved blade) resting on their necks and rocks on their jaws. This was to stop them from leaving their graves if they turned out to be vampires.*

a 1922 German movie that drew from Bram Stoker's *Dracula*, the vampire Count Orlok dies from exposure to sunlight.

FIRE, DECAPITATION, AND WOODEN STAKES THROUGH THE HEART

For pretty much the same reason they're problematic for humans, these things do not bode well for vampires.

commonly held belief that a clove of the stuff will get vampires running in the other direction.

SUNLIGHT

Vampires usually have a low tolerance for the sun. It's not that they're trying to protect their pale skin. Too much sunlight can actually kill them. In *Nosferatu*,

DRACULA: FICTION, MOSTLY

While vampires have added bite to folktales and stories for hundreds of years, today Dracula is by far the best known. He's a fictional character, but some say he has roots in reality. Bram Stoker, the writer who introduced Dracula in 1897, may have chosen the name based on a real prince named Vlad Tepes, otherwise known as Vlad the Impaler, and sometimes Dracula (see page 161).

Vlad the Impaler, aka Dracula.

Good ol' Vlad wasn't an *actual* vampire, but he was perhaps even more scary. He ruled Transylvania (now Romania) in the 1400s and he did not like to be criticized. Anyone who spoke out against him was immediately killed, and the end was not pretty. One of Vlad's more gruesome methods of doing away with enemies was to impale them on spikes—hence his nickname, "the Impaler."

Vlad's father was called Vlad Dracul, and later in life, Vlad the younger took a similar name—Vlad Dracula—for himself. While many know Vlad as a brutal, ruthless ruler, not everyone shudders when they hear his name. He is considered a hero by many Romanians because he protected the country from countless invaders.

A WORLD OF VAMPIRES

These legendary bloodsuckers from around the globe might make you want to stay close to home.

CHINA: KUANG-SHI

Tall and threatening, the Kuang-Shi is a violent demon that takes over an intact corpse—giving it claws, fangs, and scary red eyes—and then heads out to feed on the blood of human victims. If the Kuang-Shi gets enough human

blood, it becomes extra powerful and is able to fly and make itself invisible.

IRELAND: DEARG-DUE

Legend has it that Dearg-Due was a beautiful, kind woman stuck in a bad marriage. Tragically, she killed herself and now, once a year, her spirit drinks the blood of humans, especially children and young men. Some people believe she can be kept away—for one year at a time—if stones are placed over her grave.

ROMANIA: VARACOLACI

The Varacolaci is an especially greedy vampire that drinks all of its victims' blood—not just a sample. And the Varacolaci doesn't leave a wound, so there's no way for others to know it has struck. It often appears as a pale human but it can turn itself into a small animal or insect in order to sneak away after draining a victim dry. Another interesting fact: This vampire has the ability to bring on solar and lunar eclipses, some say by swallowing the sun and the moon.

RUSSIA: UPYR

The Upyr is a vicious vampire that doesn't wait for sundown to get a move on. Unlike many vampires, this one is not bothered by sunlight. While a stake to the

heart (and some holy water) will annihilate this creature, slayers should be careful not to stake the Upyr twice, as the second strike will bring it back to life.

TOGO AND GHANA: ADZE

This shape-shifting creature disguises itself as a firefly or other harmless insect and feeds on the blood of the innocent, especially children and babies. It can be destroyed only in its human form.

SURINAM: AZEMAN

During the day, this vampire looks and behaves like a regular woman. At night, she turns into a bloodsucking creature, often a bat, and looks for human victims. The Azeman is obsessed with counting, and one way to protect yourself from it is to throw lots of seeds outside your doors and windows at sundown. If all goes well, the Azeman will stay busy counting seeds until sunrise, when it turns back into a woman.

VAMPIRE ANIMALS

While vampires themselves are purely legendary, some animals with vampirelike traits are very real. Here are a few.

VAMPIRE FINCH

This bird lives in the Galápagos Islands off the coast of South America. It feeds on birds called boobies. The vampire finch pecks at the booby's body and sucks its blood without any protest from the victim, who manages to survive the feedings.

VAMPIRE FISH

Several sharp-toothed fish have earned the nickname of "vampire fish," but the payara, found in the Amazon and Orinoco River regions of Brazil and Venezuela, seems most deserving. This fish can grow to be about four feet long. Its sharp, long fangs come in handy when it goes after one of its favorite meals: the piranha, which is famous for its own set of sharp teeth and its voracious appetite for meat.

VAMPIRE MOTH

This moth, recently discovered in Siberia, sucks the blood of mammals. The insect has sharp hooks on its tongue, which it uses to puncture the skin of its victims before slurping up its meal.

WEREWOLVES

FRIGHT METER

Next time there's a full moon, listen for some mournful howling in the distance. If you feel the hairs on the back of your neck stand on end, it just might be a werewolf you are hearing.

FIVE WAYS TO BECOME A WEREWOLF

1. Get bitten by a werewolf.
2. Drink rainwater collected in the paw print of a werewolf.
3. Be cursed by a witch.
4. Dress in wolfskin.
5. Be born a werewolf (most likely to happen during a new moon).

Legend has it that a person turns into a werewolf after being bitten by one. The quick transformation happens during a full moon, and it's horrifying. Hair grows everywhere on the person's body, claws emerge on his or her fingers, and fangs appear in the mouth. Within minutes, the person has turned into a wolflike creature with sharp senses and a big appetite.

Werewolves are fast. And they're hungry—so hungry they attack humans and even eat babies and corpses. They're also usually miserable. Most werewolves are desperate to return to their human state. But until the full moon is over, there's nothing they can do. And for some, not even the moon can help: Once they become a werewolf, it's permanent. Either way, werewolves have no self-control when it comes to attacking humans. So if you see one, cross the street—fast!

HOW TO STOP A WEREWOLF

Most people believe that shooting a werewolf with a silver bullet is one of the only ways—if not *the* only way—to end its life. If you don't want to kill the werewolf, but wouldn't mind slowing it down or making it powerless for a little while, try throwing some rye, mistletoe, or a branch of a tree called mountain ash its way instead.

THE FIRST FURIOUS FURBALLS

Stories about werewolves date back to around 600 BC, when the Greek poet Homer wrote his epic poem the *Odyssey.* In this classic tale, a not-so-nice goddess named Circe transforms unsuspecting men into wolflike creatures who keep some of their human traits.

The ancient Greeks had another version of a werewolf, called a lycanthrope. It shows up in a long poem written by Ovid in AD 8, called *Metamorphoses,* or *The Book of Transformations.* The god Zeus turns King Lycaon into a wolf, making him one of the first werewolves on record.

WITCHES

FRIGHT METER

Witches have been scaring people around the world for thousands of years. Some, like the classic hook-nosed old woman in a pointy hat who eats children, appear in stories. Others are real people in history who were accused of practicing witchcraft and suffered horribly for it. Here are just a few of the wickedest witches—and witch hunters—ever.

CAN MEN BE WITCHES?

In stories and fairy tales, witches are usually women. When men practice witchcraft, they are often called warlocks, wizards, or sorcerers.

LEGENDARY WITCHES TO WATCH OUT FOR

These mythical witches have put spells on kids *and* adults all around the world.

WATER WARNING

Legend has it that a green-toothed woman, appropriately named Jenny Greenteeth, skulks along just below the surface of lakes and ponds throughout Great Britain. She waits for children and old people to pass by and then reaches out and grabs them so forcefully that her long nails puncture their skin. Some people believe that the idea for Jenny Greenteeth came out of a fear of duckweed, an invasive underwater plant. Parents would warn their children about Jenny to scare them away from the water's edge.

A TASTE FOR BLOOD

Bruxa is a Portuguese witch with a vampirelike habit: She likes to drink the blood of infants. Parents try to foil her by sewing garlic into their babies' clothes. They know when to expect her, because Bruxa keeps very precise hours: She is most likely to visit a family between midnight and 2 a.m. on Tuesdays and Fridays. But it's hard to know if she's arrived because she often disguises herself as a duck, rat, or other small animal. Legend says that after a visit from Bruxa, parents should wash their infants' clothes in boiling water and jab the garments with something sharp, a sensation Bruxa herself can feel.

WHOOO ARE YOU CALLING A WITCH?

Imagine an owl the size of a person, with a woman's face. Now you know what La Lechuza, the best-known witch in Mexico and southern Texas, looks like. Some say La Lechuza is a woman who takes the form of a bird at night. Others say she got turned into a bird as punishment for practicing witchcraft. La Lechuza attacks people who have had too much alcohol to drink. She lures them over to her by imitating a baby. She also has the power to create storms. In 2012, a photo of a larger-than-life owl surfaced on the internet and some people said it proved that La Lechuza is real.

BABA YAGA

The Russian witch Baba Yaga has many disguises. She can appear as a cloud, a moon, an animal, or even an entire season: winter. In her human form, Baba Yaga is usually an old woman who has teeth made of iron and a very long nose (see page 186). She travels on a giant mortar and pestle. If you cross her, she will likely eat you, and possibly use your remains to decorate the fence made of bones and skulls that surrounds her hut.

THE BELL WITCH

One day in 1817, a Tennessee man named John Bell spotted an animal in his field that had the body of a dog and the head of a rabbit. Fearing the strange creature, he tried to shoot it, but the animal disappeared. From then on, Bell and his family were tormented night after night by a spirit that became known as the Bell Witch. The witch would scream and chant, yank off bed-sheets, and sometimes even hit a sleeping child. When Bell died, the Bell Witch took credit. It appeared before his family and proudly announced that it had poisoned Bell the day before.

MOUSE IN THE HOUSE

Hideous-looking witches are scary, but a witch that looks like a regular person is even more terrifying. How can you even know when she is lurking nearby? In Roald Dahl's *The Witches*, the Grand High Witch and her evil cohorts don't look a thing like witches, but they have hatched a devious plan for doing away with children. They give kids treats that contain a substance that will turn them into mice, knowing that the kids' teachers will then unintentionally kill them with mouse poison to rid their classrooms of vermin. These witches give new meaning to the rule that you should never accept treats from strangers.

WICKED WITCH HUNTS

Real people have been accused of being witches throughout history. In some cases, the supposed "witch" had broken a law, but more often the accused was someone who just acted a little odd or who didn't follow the religion or the rules of those in power.

During the witch hunts that took place in Europe from 1400 to 1800, as many as 100,000 people were hanged or burned at the stake for "witchlike behavior." That could include anything from practicing a non-Christian religion to having an unexplained sickness or seizures to really any behavior not considered "normal." Unfortunately, accusing people of witchcraft was one of the traditions English settlers brought with them to America. Salem, Massachusetts, became especially famous for its brutal witch hunts.

CRUEL AND UNUSUAL PUNISHMENT

In 1692, Salem was a tight-knit community run by Puritans who had very strict ideas about religion and how people should behave. One day, two Puritan girls started acting strangely. They had screaming fits and their bodies went into physical contortions. A doctor was called in to examine them, and he decided the girls were bewitched. The girls claimed that their caretaker, a slave named Tituba, had cast a spell on them, and that set off a massive witch hunt.

A "bewitched" young woman convulsing on a courthouse floor in Salem, as the woman she accuses stands trial.

Over the next few months, fear spread through Salem like wildfire, and one person after another was accused of practicing witchcraft. They were tried in court and given

painful and sometimes fatal "tests" to determine whether or not they were witches. The accused would be thrown in water. If the person floated, that was "proof" he or she was a witch, and death or imprisonment followed. People who sank were considered innocent, but a lot of good that did once they'd drowned!

In another cruel test, extremely heavy rocks were piled on top of the suspected witch until he or she confessed. In the case of Giles Corey, this approach proved ineffective but deadly. Corey refused to declare guilt or innocence and was slowly crushed to death.

Eventually, more than 100 women, men, and children in Salem were branded "witches." About 20 of them were executed and the rest, including Tituba, were thrown in jail or publicly shamed.

Some 300 years after the mass hysteria at Salem, the reason for the two girls' bizarre behavior continues to be debated. Some historians think their convulsions were caused by food poisoning or another illness; others think they were simply playing a game. One thing is certain: They were *not* under a witch's spell.

WRITE YOUR OWN GHOST STORY

S ometimes the scariest ghost stories are the ones we invent ourselves. Here are some tips on how to make up your own.

HORRIFYING HOW-TO

- Choose a place for your ghostly encounter. It could be at night in your bedroom, or in a place that's less typical for a ghost story, like the bathroom at your school.

- Choose a time. It's best to make your story something that happened recently—last week or even yesterday. That makes it much scarier.

- When you begin telling the story, it helps to act as if you are someone who doesn't even believe in ghosts. You can say, "I've never believed in ghosts.

But what happened . . . I just can't explain it. . . ." That will make the story more convincing and make your listeners want to hear more.

- As you tell the story, make everything *almost* normal. Just change a few details so there's a feeling that something is out of the ordinary—maybe you hear a weird scratching sound, or one of the faucets in the school bathroom turns on by itself.

- Consider making the ghost in your story look like someone you know (even yourself!) but with something changed— the eyes are two different colors, or the hands are transparent.

- If you want, come up with a reason why the ghost has come back to the world of the living. Maybe the ghost is looking for something or someone, or is angry about a certain event. You don't have to be direct about this reason, but you can hint at it.

- Slowly build up to the climax of your story, where you interact with the ghost. It doesn't have to be gory— sometimes the scariest ghost just says one word, or your name, or keeps pointing at something, or just brushes by you and disappears.

- For extra creepiness, you can show your listeners a mark on your arm or something that the ghost altered in the room you're in and say, "I wouldn't have believed it if I hadn't seen this."

- At the end, hint that you don't think this ghost is gone for good. "I'm not going near that room, and I wouldn't if I were you."

XYLOPHOBIA

Xylophobia sounds like it means "fear of xylophones," but it really means a "fear of forests." Anyone who has ever read a fairy tale or gotten lost in the woods knows that there is plenty to be scared of in a forest, especially if you let your imagination run wild. From witches and goblins to wolves and bears, the deep, dark woods have a history of scaring people.

If you are just a little bit afraid of the woods and like to get off the trails before dark, you don't have xylophobia. The word applies only to an *extreme* fear of forests (and wooden objects).

Here are four real forests to avoid . . . or explore, if you dare!

PLUCKLEY SCREAMING WOODS

WHERE: Pluckley, England

WHAT'S SO SCARY: Legend has it that people passing by this forest—which happens to be in the "most haunted village in Britain"—can hear the screams of those who have died there. It is also known as Dering Woods.

OLD HOUSE WOODS

WHERE: Mathews County, Virginia, United States

WHAT'S SO SCARY: This forest is near an old port town on the coast of Virginia. There is no river running through it, which makes it very strange that people have reported seeing an old ship floating by in the fog at the edge of the woods. Some say the ship contains the ghosts of headless pirates looking for their old treasures.

DOW HILL

WHERE: Kurseong, West Bengal, India

WHAT'S SO SCARY: Located near a school that's said to be haunted, this forest has been the site of many murders. Woodcutters have reported seeing a headless boy roaming the woods.

BALLYBOLEY FOREST

WHERE: Larne, Northern Ireland

WHAT'S SO SCARY: Many superstitions and creepy stories are associated with these woods. Visitors claim they have seen shadowy figures standing still and felt like they were being watched. Some say they have heard screams that could not be traced. One man claimed he found several trees smeared with blood.

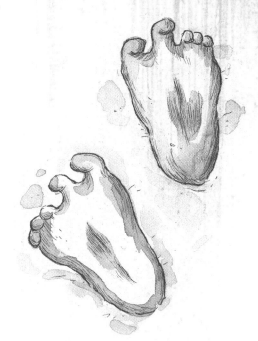

YETI

FRIGHT METER

The shaggy, apelike Yeti is one of the world's most famous cryptids—mysterious and bizarre creatures people claim to have seen but that are unknown to science. People who live in the Himalaya Mountains of Tibet and Nepal have told stories about the Yeti for centuries, describing the tall, hairy creature as part ape, part bear, and part human. (The word *yeti* comes from the Tibetan word *yeh-teh,* which means "little manlike animal.")

Reports of sightings date back to the 1800s, and descriptions of the elusive creature can make him sound not just hairy, but scary. Some claim he may weigh as much as 400 pounds and appears to be extremely strong. According to legend, the beast can lift large stones with one arm and use them as weapons. So far no one has gotten close enough to find out if that is true—or whether the Yeti really exists at all. The search for the fearsome fellow continues, though, throughout Asia and Russia.

MYSTERIOUS SIGHTINGS

Scientists say that most reports of Yeti sightings are not credible, but for decades many people have claimed they've spotted the creature or found evidence that he exists. Here are a few of the reports:

- In 1958, a Russian doctor visiting the Pamir Mountains in Central Asia said he saw a hairy, manlike creature not just once but twice in a short span of time.

- Nine American students were killed during a hiking trip deep in the mountains of Russia in 1959. Their bodies were found outside their tent, some with serious injuries. The cause

THE ABOMINABLE SNOWMAN

The Yeti is also sometimes called the Abominable Snowman, a name that came about by accident. In 1921, an explorer on an expedition in the Himalayas discovered enormous footprints. Local Sherpa guides said the prints were evidence of *metoh-kangmi*, which means "man-bear-snowman" in Tibetan. A journalist made a mistake in the translation. He reported that the term meant "dirty men/man in the snow," and dubbed the creature the Abominable Snowman. The Yeti then found itself with a new nickname.

of their deaths was never confirmed, but suspicion of a mysterious creature's involvement grew when humanlike footprints were spotted heading away from the tent. While dozens of theories abound, some people, including explorer Mike Libecki, have speculated that the Yeti is to blame.

- In the 1970s, a French mountaineer climbing in the Himalayas said that when he heard mysterious footsteps nearby, he peered through his binoculars and saw what he thought might be a Yeti. He said that he tracked it for 20 minutes.

THE BOY WHO CRIED YETI

Some claim to have seen and photographed the Yeti, but skeptics say they were actually looking at a rock or other large object, not a strange creature. In a few cases, Yeti-spotters turned out to be victims or perpetrators of elaborate hoaxes.

In winter 2013, *The Siberian Times* reported that an 11-year-old boy had found Yeti tracks on the outskirts of his village in the Russian region of Siberia. The boy and his friends followed the huge footprints to a wooded area where they claimed they met up with the real-life Yeti.

To "prove" it, one of the boys took a video on his phone to record their trek through the woods. When they got close to the supposed Yeti, they got scared. One boy shouted in Russian, "I am the nearest; I'm going to be eaten!" and they quickly ran away in the other direction.

It turned out later that animal hairs found at the site belonged to a horse, a raccoon, and a bear—but not the Yeti. Most people believe that the boys' adventure was a (mostly) well-planned hoax.

YOUR BIGGEST FEAR

What scares you the most? Find out by filling in the chart on the next page. Eight pairs of scary things from *Frightlopedia* are listed on each side of the chart. For every pair, decide which is the most frightening to you, and write your choice in the next blank. Keep going until you have your number one fear.

- Being chased by a horse-headed bat-dragon
- Being chased by a mad zombie

- A vampire bat on your pillow
- A giant scorpion on your pillow

- A spiderweb the size of four soccer fields
- An island with 4,000 venomous snakes

- Being trapped in a cave with cockroaches, bats, and rats
- Being stuck in an elevator for two days

- Being alone in a room with 2,000 mummies
- Being alone in a room with 40 venomous snakes

- A spider laying eggs in your ear
- 40,000 killer bees swarming you

- A plant that eats flesh
- A plant with fruit that explodes like dynamite

- Finding a live rat in the toilet
- Finding a live alligator in the bathtub

YOU

BIGGEST FEAR!

FEAR!

- A three-headed dog with a mane of snakes
- A living, severed hand covered with hair

- A five-foot red worm that spits acid
- A hairless lizard that paralyzes you with its gaze

- A witch that drinks babies' blood
- A ghost that knocks on your door every night

- Being bitten by a werewolf
- Being bitten by a vampire

- Swimming with a shark
- Being locked in a graveyard at night

- A jellyfish on your face
- A rattlesnake on your foot

- An alien spaceship landing in your yard
- A ghost chicken screeching at you

- An evil doll that whispers your name
- A chair that moves by itself at night

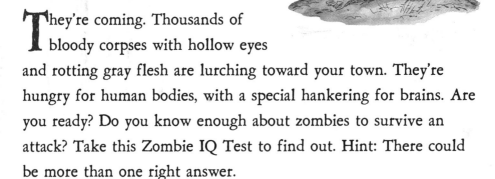

ZOMBIES

FRIGHT METER

They're coming. Thousands of bloody corpses with hollow eyes and rotting gray flesh are lurching toward your town. They're hungry for human bodies, with a special hankering for brains. Are you ready? Do you know enough about zombies to survive an attack? Take this Zombie IQ Test to find out. Hint: There could be more than one right answer.

1. Which of the following are signs that the mob of creatures chasing you are zombies?
    A. You hear moaning and groaning.
    B. You hear lots of loud talking.
    C. You notice that they stop at every intersection and look both ways before crossing.
    D. You smell something rotting.

2. If a zombie gets close to you, you should:

  A. Tell him a very sad story—he will become so upset he won't be able to attack.

  B. Throw something sharp at him. The pain will stop him in his tracks.

  C. Run.

3. A zombie has made it to your front doorstep. You crack the door open and toss him:

  A. A head of garlic.

  B. A very salty piece of meat.

  C. A note that reads, "We're not home right now, but the neighbors are."

4. The best way to kill a zombie is to:

  A. Throw him in a lake or pool and drown him.

  B. Bury him.

  C. Remove his or her clothes. Zombies can literally die of embarrassment.

  D. None of the above.

ANSWERS:

1. A and D. Zombies are terrible conversationalists. In fact, most can't talk. But they do moan and groan. They are relentlessly aggressive in their search for human flesh, which means they don't bother stopping at intersections. And because they are rotting corpses, they have major body odor issues.

2. **C.** Zombies are not terribly tender or emotional, so a sad story won't stop them. And they cannot feel pain, so a sharp instrument won't help much. But they can *inflict* pain. Better run.

3. **B.** According to folklore, when a zombie eats salt, his soul returns and he goes back to the grave, which means he will stop bothering you. This isn't true for *all* zombies, but maybe you'll be lucky. As for garlic, it protects against vampires, remember? And don't bother with notes. Zombies can't read.

4. **D.** Some zombies can be killed if you manage to destroy their brains. But in general, you can't kill (or embarrass) a zombie, because zombies are already dead.

Did you pass the quiz? If not, don't worry. Zombies are probably not about to invade your town. But zombies *have* invaded movies, TV, books, and even math lessons in some schools.

Zombies are dead bodies that have been brought back to life, usually by an outside force like a virus or radiation or a bite from another zombie. Zombies don't have minds or personalities—they can't think or talk or feel. But they *do* have goals. Actually, just one goal: eating the flesh of the living. And they won't stop until they get what they want.

This describes the zombies we know and fear today. But where did the idea of the walking dead get started? And is there such a thing as a real zombie?

ZOMBIE BEGINNINGS

Stories about corpses that come back to life have been around for thousands of years. In Chinese mythology, the undead are *jiang shi*—stiff-limbed creatures with greenish skin that kill people and suck out their *qi,* or life force. In Scandinavian tales from the eighth century, *draugr* were dead warriors that rose from the grave possessing superhuman strength and an appetite for eating their human victims whole.

Modern zombies got their start in the religious traditions of Haiti, a country in the Caribbean. During the 1700s, slaves who were brought to Haiti from West Africa practiced a religion called vodun, or voodoo, which still exists today. Most voodoo priests use their powers for good, to help people, but legend has it that a few evil priests, called *bokors,* sometimes use their powers to turn people into zombies to punish or control them. The *bokor* casts a spell on a person using a special powder. It makes the person lose his or her soul and appear to die. After burial, the *bokor* secretly returns, unearths the body, and brings it "back to life" as a zombie—someone with no mind or free will who does whatever the *bokor* says.

According to Haitian folklore, the way to release people from a zombie state is to feed them salt or have them gaze at the ocean, which lets their mind return.

REAL ZOMBIES?

For centuries, Haitians have told stories about zombies, but they didn't write them down and it's hard to know for sure if they were true. In the early 1900s, visitors to Haiti began describing encounters with zombies that *seemed* real. The American author Zora Neale Hurston wrote about a woman whose son died. A few weeks later, she saw him at work loading a truck. She called his name but he looked at her without recognizing her and said nothing. She was convinced he had been turned into a zombie. Another story described a woman with a "blank face" and "dead eyes" who walked up to a farmhouse 29 years after her death. Her brother, who still lived in the house, recognized her as his sister, but she had no idea who he was.

The word zombie *is believed to come from West Africa, where it was originally the name of a snake god. Later the word came to mean "reanimated corpse."*

Were these stories true? In the 1980s, a scientist named Wade Davis went to Haiti to try to find out. He knew that it's scientifically impossible to bring someone back from the dead, but he thought something else might be happening. He studied some "zombie powder" given to him by a voodoo sorcerer. He discovered that it contained a poison called tetrodotoxin that is found in a fish called the puffer fish. In large doses, tetrodotoxin can kill a person, but Davis thought that perhaps a smaller amount could put people in a zombielike state without killing them. Some people think Davis's theory is correct and explains how "real" zombies can exist, but others disagree.

One thing is certain: The flesh-eating creatures we picture when we hear the word *zombie* are *not* real. They have come from the very active imaginations of writers and filmmakers.

A QUICK GUIDE TO MODERN ZOMBIES

Fictional zombies have certain things in common—they are undead, they cannot remember their former selves, and they eat human flesh. But not all zombies are the same. This guide to the walking dead could help you in case of an attack.

THE "NIGHT" ZOMBIE

Named for the movie that first made zombies popular, *The Night of the Living Dead,* these zombies are often created by a mysterious form of radiation. These guys are not fussy eaters: They attack and devour anything that crosses their path, from insects to animals to humans. They are very slow and uncoordinated, but there is power in numbers, and they attack in large groups. The only way to get rid of them is to destroy their brains or set them on fire.

THE CHEMICAL ZOMBIE

These zombies first appeared in the movie *Return of the Living Dead,* and as their name suggests, they were created by a chemical spill. Unlike almost all other

Some zombies may walk slowly, but they devour human flesh quickly.

zombies, they can talk and often move very fast. Instead of eating flesh, they dine exclusively on brains. The only way to get rid of chemical zombies is to completely destroy the entire creature— usually by setting it on fire.

THE VIRAL ZOMBIE

A virus is responsible for creating this type of zombie, which then goes around biting and infecting the living. The victim dies from the virus and then comes back as a zombie. Viral zombies can multiply at an alarming rate and take over entire planets. To kill a viral zombie, you must destroy its brain.

THE SCIENCE-FICTION ZOMBIE

These zombies usually come from the labs of "scientists" who spend their days experimenting with viruses or trying to grow creatures from the cells of dead people. In a book by horror author Stephen King, cell phones turn people into zombies by wiping users' brains clean. Some science-fiction zombies look like traditional zombies, with rotting flesh and the usual signs of decay, but often they are mutated, freakish creatures. Demolishing their brains usually kills them.

THE RUNNER ZOMBIE

Unlike the classic zombie that shuffles along very slowly, dripping blood as it lurches toward a victim, these zombies are very fast and very strong. They are often created by experiments with viruses and can be hard to identify at first because they often look just like regular humans. However, when you see one leap through a window or tear apart a house, you'll know something is not quite right. Most can be stopped with a shot to the brain.

ZOMBIE ANIMALS

As far as we know, there is no such thing as a real zombie. But in the animal world, there are some creatures that come very close. Meet two of them.

FIRE ANT–DECAPITATING FLY

A soon-to-be zombified ant.

This fly uses a needle-shaped organ to lay its eggs inside a living fire ant's body.

When the fly egg hatches, the larva travels to the ant's brain and eats it. At that point, you would expect the ant to die or stop functioning, but the larva now controls it and makes it work as usual . . . for a while. When the larva matures into a pupa and is ready to become a fly, it directs the ant to travel to a bed of leaves on the forest floor where the fly emerges from the ant's empty head and zooms off.

EMERALD COCKROACH WASP

This small wasp makes a much bigger cockroach its zombie babysitter. The wasp stings the roach twice, which paralyzes the big guy's front legs and disables the escape reflex in its brain. Next the wasp bites off half of the cockroach's antennae and uses what's left to guide the roach to a nest. There, the wasp lays an egg on the roach's stomach and leaves. When the egg hatches, it feeds off the roach until it becomes a larva. Then it builds a cocoon inside the roach's body and stays there until it's an adult.

ZOMBIFY YOURSELF

FRIGHT METER

Want to look like a zombie? Makeup artist Ramy is an expert at turning people into zombies (temporarily). Use these tips to scare the daylights out of your friends and family at Halloween, or whenever you feel like impersonating the living dead.

HORRIFYING HOW-TO

WHAT YOU NEED

- White face makeup
- Black face makeup
- Blue face makeup (optional)
- Fake blood (optional; see page 40)
- Applicator (optional)
- An adult to help

WHAT YOU DO

1. Using your fingers, apply the white makeup to your entire face—your forehead, nose, cheeks, chin—and also your neck. Avoid your eye area. Blend the makeup well so that it looks even, light, and uniform.

2. Using your fingers or an applicator, add the black makeup around your eyes—from your eyelids all the way up to your eyebrows, and under your eyes so that your entire eye is surrounded by black. Be careful. Don't get any makeup in your eyes.

3. Suck in your cheeks and apply black makeup to the hollows of your cheeks (just underneath your cheekbones), blending the makeup up and down to give your face a sunken-in look. (To look extra creepy, add a bit of black makeup to your lips.)

4. If you have blue makeup, dip your index finger into it and draw very thin, squiggly vertical lines on your forehead and chin. Blend it in so that the blue is very faint. This should look like veins peeking through your zombified skin.

5. If want to look like you just had a snack of the human variety, make some fake blood (see page 40) and smear it on your chin, neck, and around your mouth.

Note: If you don't have white, black, or blue face makeup, you can still be a zombie! Ask an adult for help, and use the following materials:

- **For white face makeup**, try a foundation, concealer, or powder that's significantly lighter than your own skin tone.
- In place of **black and blue face makeup**, use black or blue eye shadow.

PHOTO CREDITS